Mormons and Muslims: A Case of Matching Fingerprints

Mormons and Muslims are More Alike than You Might Think

by

Dennis Kirkland

Xulon
PRESS

Paul,

I am Jord C...

Thank you for your help and encouragement along the way. It has been my joy to serve as a co-teacher with you @ MHBC.

Thanks for serving

Let's keep serving together.

I love you in the Lord!

Your Brother & Friend,

Dennis Kirkland

phil 1:6

#8of10

Mormons and Muslims: A Case of Matching Fingerprints
Mormons and Muslims are More Alike than You Might Think
by Dennis Kirkland

Printed in the United States of America

ISBN 978-1-60477-760-4

www.xulonpress.com

Dedication

To my loving wife, Lora, and my children,
Daniel, Paul, Abigail, Deborah, Joseph, and Nathan.
I love you. I bless you. I give you to God.

—

To my under-appreciated Mother-in-Law, Janice
Makemson, I am deeply indebted to you for the many hours
of tedious editing. I could not have done it without you.
Thanks Jan.

About the Author

DENNIS KIRKLAND is a former Marine Infantryman (E-5). He and his wife, Lora, have been missionaries for over 20 years. He has been Professor of Missions at Appalachian Bible College, Beckley, West Virginia since 2004. He teaches Missions and World Religions at ABC and serves as adjunct faculty for a local, non-Christian university teaching Religion and Philosophy. He served as a missionary pastor in Puerto Rico and in Richfield, Utah before becoming a college teacher. His specialties include Expository Preaching, Worldviews, and Philosophical Logic. He is a sky and SCUBA diver, a pilot, a ham, a guitarist, and hunts when he can. He is a member of the International Society of Christian Apologetics. He holds a BA in Missions (88) and an MA in Theology (96) from Southeastern Bible College (Birmingham, AL). He holds an MA in Biblical Studies (05, Honors) from Temple Baptist Theological Seminary (Chattanooga, TN). His doctorate (DMin, anticipated 08) is from Liberty Baptist Theological Seminary (Lynchburg, VA).

Acknowledgements

Past and present students at Appalachian Bible College—
I love you guys.
Go serve Him!

(Prospective students can check out Appalachian Bible
College at www.abc.edu.)

Dr. David E. Bouler, Jack Davis, Dr. John D. Talley, Jr.,—
Dr. John C. Wecks and Dr. James D. Price—
Every day in the ministry harness
deepens my appreciation for your input into my life.
Thanks!

Table of Contents

Chapter 1 – CSI: Comparing, Studying, Investigating 11
    Why Mormons and Muslims?...............................11

Chapter 2 – Dusting for Fingerprints...19
    Uncovering Uncommonly Common
        Common Denominators....................................19
    Twenty Five Matching Fingerprints......................20
    Mormons, Muslims and a *Modus Operandi* 27

Chapter 3 – Brushing their Books for Matching Fingerprints.......31
    Can the Qur'an and the Quad BOTH be
        the Word of God?..31
        The Muslim Qur'an 33
        The Mormon Quad 43
        The Word of God 53

Chapter 4 – Lifting their Fathers' Fingerprints 61
    Is God the Father a Bad Dad?...............................61
        What kind of Dad is "Father *Allah?*" 61
        What kind of Dad is "Heavenly
        Father *Elohim?*"..73
        What kind of Dad is *"Abba?"* 83

Chapter 5 – Checking their Christs' Matching Fingerprints..........89
    Is Jesus Satan's Brother? Is Jesus Just
      Another Prophet?..89
        Who Do Muslims say that I (Jesus) Am? 89
        Who Do Mormons say that I (Jesus) Am?......98

Chapter 6 – Detecting a Fingerprint Pattern in the Afterlife........115
    Is Eternal Life Like a Box of Chocolates?...........115
      Muslim Paradise is Questionable...................116
      Mormons Have Three Heavenly Options.....121

Chapter 7 – Profiling Women for Matching Fingerprints............127
    Pregnant Virgins?!..127
      Christian Thought about Women's Issues.....128
      Muslim Thought about Women's Issues.......130
      Mormon Thought about Women's Issues 136

Chapter 8 – Contaminating the Evidence about Israel.................145
    Do they Replace Israel as God's Chosen
      People? 145
      A Biblical Perspective of Israel 146
      Mormons Tinker with Israel's Future 154
      Muslims Tamper with Israel's Past...............156

Chapter 9 – Calling Witnesses to Mormons and Muslims...........159
    The Foundation for taking the Witness Stand......160
    Ten Fingerprint Principles for Witnesses.............162

Chapter 1

CSI—Comparing, Studying, Investigating

Why Mormons and Muslims?

W hy write a book comparing Mormons and Muslims? The main reason is to inform and thereby equip Christians for their inevitable contact with these faiths and their believers. The world is truly becoming a global village, and Christians must be equipped to have meaningful conversations with "villagers" from other religions. Since the biblical Christian's hope is to use personal contact to point others to Jesus Christ as the only true Savior, knowledge of Muslim and Mormon beliefs will help prepare the Christian for such conversations. The Apostle Paul is a biblical example. Acts 17 records his dialog with religious men of his day who subscribed to a different faith. Paul was obviously well aware of what these religious philosophers believed, and as a result he was able to have meaningful conversation with them and point them to Jesus Christ as their only hope. Likewise, this book provides information that can help Christians have something to say to Muslims and Mormons. The information is not to be used as a spiritual club to bash Muslims or Mormons but rather as a means of better understanding and identifying their needs, which can be met only in Jesus!

A second and broader reason for such a book is to inform any reader, Christian or non-Christian. Everyone would profit by knowing something of what Mormons and Muslims believe. America is becoming more diverse. Muslims are becoming a common part of the social and political scene, and they should be welcomed! Every American needs to understand Muslim thought. Likewise, family-friendly Mormon commercials are common on American television. It is possible that a future President of the United States could be Mormon. Americans need to understand how Mormons view important issues. This book will help any member of the global community better understand the values and beliefs behind these rising social, religious, and political powers.

Comparing Muslims and Mormons is Not New

Making a comparison between Muslims and Mormons is not new. Since the founding of Mormonism in the early 1800's, several comparisons have been made. The comparisons have come from three camps. They are the secular, non-Christian; the Mormon; and the Evangelical Christian.

Secular Comparison

A German historian, Eduard Meyer (1855-1930), made a major comparison between the two religions. A quick web search tells us that Eduard Meyer was one of the most learned men of modern times. He was not a Christian. Ancient history was his specialty. Particularly interested in the how religions began, his massive writings include works on the origin of religions. Meyer even spent a year in Utah to study the Latter-day Saints (Mormons). He was also well versed in Islam and noted that Mormons and Muslims resemble each other in many ways. His comparison book was originally titled *Ursprung and Geschichte der Mormonen* (Halle: Niemeyer, 1912). It was translated from German by H. Rahde and E. Seaich and published again as *The Origin and History of the Mormons* (Salt Lake City: University of Utah, 1961). Even this secular history says,

"Of the many new religious movements originating in our time, Mormonism very early awakened my interest, especially because of its surprising and close resemblance to the historical development of Islam.

Without the least exaggeration, we may designate the Mormons as the Mohammedans of the New World according to their origins and their manner of thinking. There is hardly a historical parallel which is so instructive as this one; and through comparative analysis both receive so much light that a scientific study of the one through the other is indispensable."

A second non-Christian comparison is in a section of the book *History of the Saints: An Exposé of Joe Smith and Mormonism* written in 1842 by John C. Bennet. John Bennet was a former Mormon who had been dis-fellowshipped by the Church of Jesus Christ of Latter-day Saints(LDS). He had been a celebrated Mormon "insider." For a time, he was second only to Joseph Smith. His knowledge of the LDS church makes his comparison both credible and striking.

Another book, *The City of the Saints*, was written in 1861 by Richard Francis Burton. Burton had a vast knowledge of Islam from his military service in Asia and India. For him, the comparison between Muslim and Mormon belief was clear and easy. He saw the matching fingerprints.

In 1906 Jennie Fowler Willing published *Mormonism: The Mohammedanism of the West*, and in 1912 Bruce Kinney wrote a book entitled *Mormonism: The Islam of America*. As the reader can see, comparing Muslims and Mormons is not a new idea. But it is one that needs refreshing in our time of pluralism and tolerance.

Mormon Comparison

Interestingly, there are also two books written from a Mormon point of view that make a direct comparison between the two faiths. The first is a book called *The Correlation of Muslim Doctrine and Latter-day Saint Doctrine Based on the Holy Scriptures* by Amos R. Jackson. This book was published by Mr. Jackson's widow several years after his death. The Jackson family was a devout Mormon family. In the 1960's they hosted a young Muslim from Indonesia as an exchange student. This young man's religious devotion attracted Jackson's attention. Jackson noticed the matching fingerprints and made a comparison of the two faiths based on their scriptures which he simply categorized and quoted side-by-side. Mr. Jackson writes,

"As I studied the Qur'an, with all the commentaries and notes, I noted significant doctrinal concepts that are clearly corollary to those found in the accepted Scriptures of The Church of Jesus Christ of Latter-day Saints."

His book contains comparative quotes from the Old and New Testaments, the Book of Mormon, and the Qur'an (KUR-an), on Jesus Christ, Mary, Atonement, Plan of Salvation, Prophets, Priesthood, Covenant Peoples, and Prayer. He says,

"It is my humble prayer that this undertaking might be a source of greater love and understanding between two great peoples who diligently seek to know God and the Prophets he has sent to give us guidance."

A second book that compares the two faiths from a Mormon point of view is *Mormons and Muslims: Spiritual Foundations and Modern Manifestations* edited by Spencer J. Palmer. This is a most interesting volume! It is a publication of papers presented at a symposium held on the campus of Brigham Young University in October of 1981. The purpose of the symposium was to investigate the parallels, similarities, and contrasts of Muslims and Mormons. It is fascinating to see how the representatives of both religions note the matching fingerprints.

The two books written from a Mormon perspective desire to embrace the similarities. The Mormon view is positive! Mormons want to give the Muslims a hug and invite them to believe in Joseph Smith as a more modern prophet than Mohammed. This makes perfect sense to a Mormon because Mormon belief is based on the idea that God is still giving His Word to prophets today. It is not surprising to note that the Muslims are not as friendly to the idea of embracing Mormon prophets such as Joseph Smith.

Another invitation to compare these two religions came directly from the founder of Mormonism, who likened himself to Mohammed. In the charged atmosphere of the Missouri "Mormon War" of 1838, Joseph Smith said,

> "I will be to this generation a second Mohammed, whose motto in treating for peace was 'the Alcoran [Koran] or the Sword.' So shall it eventually be with us—'Joseph Smith or the Sword!'" [1]

Mormons also compare themselves to Muslims in less direct ways. One such comparison is a short theological treatise called, "*A Message of Friendship.*" It was written by David Stewart for the Foundation for Apologetic Information and Research. (It is good reading and can be accessed at *www.fairlds.org.*) The gist of the writing is that Mormons want to embrace Muslims as brothers and sisters and invite them to accept Joseph Smith as a more recent prophet. Stewart clearly points out some of the common denominators (matching fingerprints) between the two systems. The opening paragraph says,

> "Latter-day Saints recognize Muslims as brothers and sisters, children of our Heavenly Father, with whom we can find much common ground. LDS Prophet and Apostle Gordon B. Hinckley stated: 'We value our Muslim neighbors across the world.' Latter-day Saints respect the strong family values and moral accomplishments of Muslims as well as Islamic contributions to science, literature, history, philosophy, medicine, and the arts. While there are many differences between Muslims and Latter-day Saints in doctrine and practice, we acknowledge these differences with respect rather than criticism. Latter-day Saints extend a hand of friendship to Muslims everywhere." [2]

The Mormon hope seems to be that Muslims will embrace the LDS founder with the same reverence they give Mohammed.

Christian Comparison

Many think Muslims and Mormons are completely different. We contend that, theologically, they are not as far apart as you might think. While we are not saying that Mormons and Muslims are identical, we are saying they are very much alike. The resemblance is so apparent that it deserves a closer look from a Christian viewpoint. We will look at some key points of these two religions and highlight their uncanny resemblance. We will use their own scriptures and accepted authoritative sources to demonstrate the similarities. The chapters that follow reveal that the fingerprints on Mormonism and the fingerprints on Islam do match! Their likenesses will point to an inescapable conclusion — both religions are covered with matching fingerprints. Those matching fingerprints point to a common suspect — Lucifer!

False Religions Add, Subtract, Multiply, and Divide

There is a very easy way to outline a paper or a talk about cults and world religions by using four points: Add, Subtract, Multiply, and Divide. Yes, these are the basic math functions. It is possible to examine any sect, cult, or false religion using these four touch-points.

Let's do the math! Let's hang some thoughts about Muslim and Mormon beliefs on these four hooks.

- **Add** – Both religions add to the Bible by claiming to have received additional instructions (revelations) from God.
- **Subtract** – Both subtract from Jesus Christ's person and from His Work:
  o From His person by saying that Jesus was less than God.
  o From His work by saying that His death was not quite enough to make men right with God. They say their religions "take up the slack."
- **Multiply** – Both multiply the requirements for salvation.
- **Divide** – Both divide men into "believers" and "infidels."

Interestingly, both groups murdered "unbelieving infidels" on the very same date. The date is September 11. On September 11, 1857, some Mormon militiamen massacred about 140 men, women and children under the authority of Brigham Young. This incident came to be called the "Mountain Meadow Massacre" and is the subject of a motion picture made in 2007. One hundred forty-four years later, on September 11, 2001, a group of fanatical followers of Mohammed attacked the United States using hijacked airliners.

That date, September 11 (9/11), is interesting! A missionary friend who works with Muslims in Europe reminded me that 9/11 is historically significant to Muslims. The story goes back to when Muslims were advancing across Europe until they were stopped at the city of Vienna, Austria. The year was 1683. The Muslim Turks laid siege to the city. The city and possibly all of Europe was doomed if they could not break the Muslim siege. The Polish cavalry and the German infantry broke the siege on September 11. This saved Vienna and proved to be a turning point. The tide of Muslim expansion into the West that began in 632 AD started to recede. This event of September 11, 1683, effectively stopped the spread of Islam. My friend is of the opinion that Islamic militant extremists chose 9/11 as the day to attack the World Trade Center on US soil because it symbolized the renewed Islamic military expansion! Osama Bin Laden was symbolically resuming a battle that was thought to have been lost over 300 years ago. This is a very interesting thought! It should awaken the detective in all of us!

Chapter 1

Questions for Discussion

1. Why are all men religious? (Investigate Ecclesiastes 3:11.)
2. How does knowing the beliefs of other religions help Christians?
3. Is it possible to study other beliefs too much? If so, why?
4. Is it fair to compare Mormons and Muslims? Why? Why not?
5. Would you vote for a Mormon or Muslim running for the highest office of our land? Why? Why not?

Chapter 2

Dusting for Fingerprints

❖❖❖

Uncovering Uncommonly Common Common Denominators

In a recent Global Apologetics class, we were having a discussion about Islam when Dr. Ergun Caner asked, "Have you students ever thought about how much Muslims and Mormons are alike?" Before we answered he rattled off three things that are common to both religions. He paused and then started to move back to discussing Islam. I spoke up to say that the list is even longer and told him that I had noticed the similarities when I lived and worked for four years among Mormons in rural Utah. The more we talked, the more common denominators we found. Several others in the group listened with great interest. Like most Christians they were unaware of how these two religious groups are not so different.

Some might say, "Stop! They can't be alike. One religion is from Arabia and other is from America. One says God speaks Arabic and the other "Egyptian Hieroglyphics." One wears turbans and veils and the other wears dark suits, white shirts and dark ties. They can't be alike!"

There are some obvious outward differences, but when we boil it down to basic theological beliefs they are more alike than you might think.

This chapter covers some of the teachings that both groups have in common. Though not an exhaustive treatment of each teaching, it will open the door and let some light shine in. It will best serve as a starting point for your own deeper study. We begin with a list of 25 common denominators to ponder. You may be able to think of more. The more significant similarities are listed with greater detail.

Twenty-Five Sets of Matching Fingerprints

1. The founders of both religions claimed to be visited by Angels.

   • Mohammed said he was visited by an angel named Gabriel.
   • Joseph Smith said he was visited by an angel named Moroni.

2. Both men claimed supernatural experiences.

   • Mohammed claimed to be "transported" from one place to another in a supernatural way that defied the laws of space, time, and gravity.
   • Joseph Smith claimed that God the Father, Jesus, and John the Baptist appeared to him on different occasions.

   Visits from this "trinity" make his claim to have been visited regularly by the mere angel Moroni seem like a second class miracle. Nevertheless, he claimed supernatural experiences.

3. Both were told that all existing religions were false.

   • Mohammed was told that the revelation(s) ("recitations") he was given were the only truth. He was told that all the Jewish, Christian, Zoroastrian, and Buddhist teachings he heard were corruptions and lies.

- Joseph Smith heard the same idea. He was told that all the religious beliefs of his day were lies and abominations. All the churches of his day (Baptist, Methodist, Presbyterian, Congregationalist, etc.) were apostate. They had lost the truth.

4. Both leaders were told that they would restore true religion on earth.

   - In the 600's AD, Mohammed claimed to be the channel or conduit that God (Allah) would use to establish true religion. A required saying of Islam is, "There is no god but Allah, and Mohammed is his prophet."
   - Joseph Smith made the same claim in the early 1800's. Mormons today define the word "Gospel" as the "good news that the truth which had been lost was restored through Joseph."

5. Both religions teach a works salvation.

   - The Qur'an says, "Then, he whose balance (of good deeds) will be (found) heavy, Will be in a life of good pleasure and satisfaction. But he whose balance (of good deeds) will be (found) light, Will have his home in a (bottomless) Pit" (Sura 101:6-9).

     The Qur'an also states that "those who believe in Allah and work righteousness, He will admit to Gardens beneath which Rivers flow, to dwell therein for ever: Allah has indeed granted for them a most excellent Provision" (Sura 65:11)

   - The Book of Mormon teaches: "And moreover, I would desire that ye should consider on the blessed and happy state of those that keep the commandments of God. For behold, they are blessed in all things, both temporal and spiritual; and if they hold out faithful to the end they are received into heaven, that thereby they may dwell with God in a state of never-ending happiness" (Mosiah 2:41).

Second Nephi 25:23 indicates that a man is saved "by grace through faith after he has done all he can do."

The interpretation of this verse that is common among my Mormon friends is that grace and faith kick in only AFTER you have done all the works you can do. But, who could ever say, "I've done ALL I could ever do?"

6. Both founders wanted to unite the various religions/sects of their day.

   • Mohammed preached his message to the polytheists of Mecca, Saudi Arabia and wanted them to join him in his new, true religion.
   • Joseph Smith preached his message to all those around him warning them of their error and inviting them to join him. Many people of different denominations joined and still do. [1]

7. The sayings of both founders were written down and came to be viewed as "inspired" by God.

   • During fits that resembled seizures, Mohammed "recited" the sayings that were collected and later became the Qur'an.
   • Joseph Smith "translated" the Book of Mormon from behind a curtain using special "glasses" given to him by supernatural means.

8. Both rejected the Bible and said it was changed by men, corrupted, and unreliable.
9. Both claimed their holy book was the most correct and perfect book on earth.
10. Both claimed that their scripture was based upon a record stored in heaven.

- Mohammed's followers say that Allah has the original copy of the Qur'an with him in Paradise.
- Joseph Smith claimed that the angel Moroni took the golden plates back to heaven.

11. Both men claimed to be God's final prophet.

It is interesting to note that both religions are founded on prophets. Muslims believe that prophets speak for God. Their prophet was Mohammed. Mormons have responded logically to this by reaching out to Muslims and accepting them as having truth but just not having the latest edition of truth. An LDS Apostle, George Q. Cannon stated:

"I believe myself that Mohamed, whom the Christians deride and call a false prophet and stigmatize with a great many epithets—I believe that he was a man raised up by the Almighty, and inspired to a certain extent by Him to effect the reforms which he did in his land, and in the nations surrounding. He attacked idolatry, and restored the great and crowning idea that there is but one God. He taught that idea to his people, and reclaimed them from polytheism and from the heathenish practices into which they had fallen. I believe many men were inspired who lived after him and before him, who, nevertheless, did not have the Holy Priesthood, but were led by the Spirit of God to strive for a better condition of affairs and to live a purer and higher life than those by whom they were surrounded were living. But while this was the case, it was the Spirit of God that did it." (George Q. Cannon, *Journal of Discourses,* 24:371)

It seems logical that Muslims might embrace Joseph as a prophet. He made the same kind of claims as Mohammed. However, Muslims do not respond with the same tolerance that Mormon folk show them. Could part of the reason be the fact that Joseph was a white American? Some Muslims are very intolerant of anything other than Islam. They would be especially intolerant of a religion founded by a white American.

12. Both founders became military leaders.

- Mohammed became a warrior who led his followers in military strikes that were successful in taking cities.
- Joseph Smith became a Lieutenant General in the militia of his area and is said to have been very fond of wearing the uniform. He actually died in an exchange of gunfire with a murderous mob. Not that we blame him for shooting back. The mob was intent on killing him before "General Joseph's" Mormon Militia arrived.

13. Both claimed that they were persecuted because of their pure faith.
14. Both "prophets" began as monogamists but became polygamists.
15. Both borrowed other religious ideas of their day.

- Mohammed borrowed the Roman Catholic idea of pilgrim-ages as well as the Old Testament Jewish idea of central, locational worship. Each faithful Muslim aspires to make a pilgrimage to their central location, Mecca.
- Joseph Smith was eclectic in borrowing from everyone.

16. Both founders later received "corrections" to their inspired scriptures.
17. Both religions fought over who would lead after the founder died.

- Mohammed's followers divided into two major sects (Sunni, Shi'ite) after the first several caliphs (leaders) were murdered by their rivals. Yes, murdered! The dividing issue was over having a blood relative of Mohammed serve as the leader of the religion.

- Joseph Smith's followers split over those who wanted a blood relative of his to serve as leader and those who voted for Brigham Young. Brigham Young, not a relative, became the leader and moved to Utah. Those who followed Joseph's son stayed back east. This is not a huge rift, like the Muslim Sunni/Shiite rift, but it is an interesting parallel.

18. Both groups are actually ruled by <u>sayings</u> of the founders not the key inspired books.

- Islam's holy book is the Qur'an. It is a short book. It is shorter than the Bible and does not address every topic of life. However, the sayings of Mohammed were compiled by his followers into what is called the *Hadith* (or Saying). These sayings are large additional sets of books. One authority, a man named Bukari, collected and published a nine volume set of *Hadiths*. In reality, the *Hadiths*, not the Qur'an, dictate life for the Muslim. These sayings often contradict each other and make life complicated for Muslims.
- Joseph Smith supposedly continued to be God's channel as he wrote *Pearl of Great Price* and *Doctrine and Covenants*. In fact, most of the Mormon distinctive, such as Temple Rituals and Baptism for the Dead, does NOT come from the Book of Mormon. The distinctive practices and beliefs come from the later books.

19. Both religions have "fundamentalists" factions who are violent and/or anti-social.

- Mohammed has followers who fly airplanes into buildings. Others blow themselves up along with innocent women and children. We all have heard of these extremists.
- Joseph Smith has followers who live in their own secluded culture as polygamists. Some early followers even killed "infidels" traveling through Utah in the Mountain Meadow

Massacre. However, please note that Mormons value human life far more than Muslim extremists. There was only one Mountain Meadow Massacre. We hear of Muslim extremist violence almost daily.

20. Both deny that Jesus is the unique Son of God.

    • Mohammed agreed that Jesus' birth was a miracle in that He was born of a virgin. But Mohammed would elevate Jesus only to the level of prophet, like Abraham or Moses.
    • Joseph Smith taught that Jesus was the physical offspring of God the Father's physical (bodily) union with Mary.

21. Both deny that Jesus' death on the Cross is important.

    • Mohammed taught that a "body-double" was used for the Crucifixion and that Jesus did not really die on the cross.
    • Joseph Smith taught that the REAL suffering happened in the Garden of Gethsemane and not on the cross.

    Have you noticed that there are no crosses on Mormon meeting houses or temples? They de-emphasize the cross.

22. Both control the diets of their followers.

    • At breakfast, Mohammed's followers cannot have bacon with their eggs.
    • Joseph Smith's followers have to skip the coffee.

23. Both require devout followers to wear specific types of clothing.

    • Mohammed's followers require their women to wear veils and burquas.
    • Joseph Smith's followers who are devout must wear special underwear. Really!

24. Both put women on a lower level than men.

   - Mohammed taught that the witness of a woman was worth only half the weight of a witness who is a man.
   - Joseph Smith taught that a woman has no hope of eternal bliss without being married (and sealed) to a man.

25. Both have their own versions of heaven and Paradise.

   - Mohammed's Paradise is testosterone-oriented and includes harems of virgins with beautiful eyes.
   - Joseph Smith's heavens (yes, heavens–there are three) are also oriented around sexual delight, but the women are all wives and are always pregnant.

Muslims, Mormons, and Satan's Modus Operandi (M.O.)

Why are these two religions so much alike? The answer is simple. These two faiths are alike because of the enemy of Christianity — Satan. Satan does not care what you believe as long as you do not believe the truth! He is the driving force behind all non-biblical religions that turn men away from Christ.

How does Satan operate? He is a schemer and deceiver. The whole scope of Scripture paints this dark picture of him. Let's go back to the beginning. In Genesis (Old Testament) we see Satan working his deception on Adam and Eve. Adam and Eve lived in a perfect world. They had everything they needed. It was Utopia! They had no bent toward sinning. Satan rose to the challenge of ruining this perfection. He caused the whole human race (Adam and Eve) to break the whole Law of God ("Don't eat of this tree.").

In II Corinthians 11:14 (New Testament), we see Satan working to deceive church members. He disguises himself as something positive — an angel of light. His scheme is to make men and women accept him as good. Then he offers more revelation than what is contained in the Bible.

From these two passages we can see a *modus operandi* (MO). Satan schemes and deceives. He did it in the Garden of Eden, with Corinthian believers, Mohammed, Joseph Smith, and countless others. We can make five observations about how Satan works.

Satan's Operating Principles

1. Satan attacks at weak points.

In the Garden, Satan attacked Eve, not Adam. 1 Timothy 2:14 shows us that it was Eve who was deceived by Satan, not Adam. Satan's plan was to cause and use uncertainty. He found Eve alone and unfortified. Adam was either not present or not protective. When Satan found the weak point, he probed with questions to insinuate doubt. Satan causes and welcomes distress and confusion.

Notice that both Mohammed and Joseph Smith were distressed and confused by the religious talk of their day. They were ripe for new revelation. They were looking for something outside the Bible and they had mystical, supernatural experiences at times of vulnerability. Also remember that just because it is supernatural does not mean it is from God! Satan attacked them at a weak point. This is Satan's MO.

2. Satan deceives leaders who cause others to stumble.

Both Adam and Eve sinned, but Eve was deceived, Adam was not. Satan deceived a leader, in this case Eve. Others (Adam) followed the leader! In Corinth, deceivers had come and led the church to stumble. Second Corinthians 11:13-15 describes how deceitful men cause others to stumble:

> "For such men are false apostles, deceitful workers, disguising themselves as apostles of Christ. No wonder, for even Satan disguises himself as an angel of light. Therefore it is not surprising if his servants also disguise themselves as servants of righteousness, whose end will be according to their deeds."

Another passage, 2 Timothy 3:13, says,

"But evil men and impostors will proceed from bad to worse, deceiving and being deceived"

Satan's MO was to deceive a leader who would then lead others away from God. Eve led Adam away. False teachers led Corinthian believers away. Joseph and Mohammed have led multitudes away. They followed the pattern and left behind matching fingerprints.

   3. Satan questions and adds to the Word of God.

In Genesis, Satan is introduced in this way:

"Now the serpent was more crafty than any beast of the field which the LORD God had made. And he said to the woman, 'Indeed, *has God said*, "You shall not eat from any tree of the garden?" ' Genesis 3:1

He caused Eve to doubt what she already <u>knew</u> God had said. In the cases of Joseph Smith and Mohammed, the supernatural beings that appeared to them also denied and added to the Word of God!

   4. Satan attacks God's character.

In Genesis, Satan convinces Eve that God is not seeking her best interests, but is holding her back from her full potential. Further, he calls God a liar, and assures Eve that she will not surely die for disobeying God.

   6. Satan mixes error with truth.

In Genesis 3, some of what the serpent said was accurate! He also quoted Scripture when he tempted our Lord (Matthew 4:4, 6). The Scriptures he quoted were true, but Satan distorted and twisted them. He employed them in a way that made disobedience to God seem justified. The most cunning and dangerous false teachers are those who seem to embrace the Word of God, but subtly undermine it. Both Joseph and Mohammed gave the Bible a nod of approval. However, they undermined it by adding their personal revelations.

In 2 Corinthians 2:11 Paul says, "For we are not ignorant of his devices." As we proceed, we will be able to see more and more of Satan's method of operation.

Chapter Conclusion

Why are there so many similarities between Mormons and Muslims? Like a stream that divides and flows in two directions, they flow from the same headwaters of deception. Satan doesn't care what you believe as long as you DON'T believe the truth. When it comes to Muslims and Mormons, Satan used the same method of operation. As we examine them, we see Satan's fingerprints.

These two faiths share uncommonly common common denominators!

Chapter 2

Questions for Discussion

1. Are there common denominators between ALL religions?
2. Can you think of more common denominators between Mormons and Muslims?
3. How do you see Satan's *modus operandi* in other cults? Other religions?
4. Have you personally experienced Satan's attack when you were at a weak point?
5. How can you better prepare yourself for Satan's attacks?

Chapter 3

Brushing their Books for Matching Fingerprints

Can the Qur'an and the Quad Both be the Word of God?

In construction there is always a reference point from which everything is measured. If we were building a castle, each wall would be aligned to the first stone set in place. Setting that first stone, the cornerstone, impacts every other part of the building. The Qur'an is the cornerstone for Muslims. The Mormon cornerstone is the Quad. Because their 'bibles' are the foundation for all of their beliefs, we need to take time to understand the Mormon and Muslim cornerstones.

History was made in the United States of America on January 4, 2007 as a Democratic Congressman from Minnesota was sworn into office. The Congressman's name was Keith Ellison. History was made when he placed his hand upon the Holy Qur'an (KUR-an) to be sworn into office. It was the first time in the history of the United States that a congressman was sworn into such a high office using a holy book other than the Bible. Keith Ellison said, "I will put my hand on a book that is the basis of my faith, which is Islam, and I think this is a thing of beauty—a wonderful thing for our country."

Please note that he said, "I will put my hand on a book that is the basis of my faith." The basis for his faith is a book called The Holy

Qur'an. The Qur'an is the holy book, the foundational document for the religion called Islam.

The fact that this happened in the United States indicates that the culture of the United States is changing. There is no doubt that Christians in the US need to be informed and aware of the changes that are taking place. One way Christians can be informed and aware is to understand this holy book called *Qur'an.*

In 2007, a Mormon announced that he is running for president of the US. For the first time, a Mormon is a serious contender for the office. If he were elected, he could also choose to be sworn into the office using a book other than the Bible. If a Mormon is elected President of the United States, like Rep. Keith Ellison, he **could** say, "I will place my hand on a book that is the basis of my faith, which is Mormonism." What book would that be? It would not be the Bible! It would be the Book of Mormon!

A Mormon person would more likely use a book that would look much like a Bible. It would be about the size of a good study Bible like *The MacArthur Study Bible* which is less than two inches thick. It might be bound in leather with gold-edged pages. What is this book? Mormon missionaries have a nickname for it. They call it a "Quad." The nickname is Quad because *quad* means four, as in four separate items. The Mormon Quad is actually four books bound together. The Quad is made up of a *KJV Bible*, *The Book of Mormon*, *Pearl of Great Price*, and *Doctrine and Covenants*. These are known as the General Works and together are considered to be the basis for Mormonism. Mitt Romney *could* ask to be sworn in using a Quad.

My personal hope is that our culture does not move away from its biblical moorings to the point that high ranking officials no longer see the Bible as the foundation. However, either a Qur'an or a Quad could be used in place of the Bible because they, not the Bible, are the foundation stones for Muslims and Mormons. It seems inevitable that biblical Christianity is on a collision course with both the Qur'an and the Quad in the public arena. Christians need to be aware of these two holy books.

What do these two faith groups have in common when it comes to their scriptures? Much! Let's list the common denominators here.

Then as you read through the chapter you will be able to see more of the specifics about each.

Matching Fingerprints: How Muslims and Mormons view SCRIPTURE

1. The founders of both religions were told that God had additional truth to reveal.
2. Both founders claim supernatural visions while scripture was being given.
3. Both claimed their revelations were God's final revelations.
4. Both claimed that what they wrote was directly inspired by God.
5. Both rejected the Bible and said it was changed by men, corrupted, and unreliable.
6. Both claimed their holy book was the most correct and perfect book on earth.
7. Both claimed that their scripture was based upon a 'file' stored in heaven.
8. Both founders received "corrections" to their inspired scriptures.
9. Both religions have a primary revealed book, and secondary books of human sayings.

With those facts as background, let's look at these two holy books and see where they came from. Since the *Qur'an* is older than the *Quad*, let's look at it first.

The Muslim Qur'an

What is The Qur'an?

Simply stated, the Qur'an is the scripture for the religion of Islam. It is their bible. A textbook definition of the Qur'an is "the sacred scripture of the Muslims, regarded as the word of God dictated to Mohammed by God through the archangel Gabriel. The prophet received and recited the messages over approximately 20 years." [1] Another textbook defines the Qur'an as "The most important sacred text in Islam—their Holy Scripture. Muslims believe it was revealed to the prophet Mohammed piecemeal, by God and written in Arabic. All Muslims believe the Qur'an to be divine in origin." [2]

The Arabic word "Qur'an" is derived from the root "*qara'a*", which means "to read" or "to recite." This was the command which the angel Gabriel supposedly gave Mohammed. Allegedly, Gabriel first appeared to Mohammed in July of 610 AD. Mohammed was in a cave at the time. It was the *Hira* Cave located about three miles northeast of the city of Mecca.

Muslims believe that the Qur'an is the final revelation from Allah. In Arabic the Qur'an is referred to as '*Al-Kitab*' (the book); '*Al-furkan*' (the distinction); and '*Al-dikhr*' (the warning).

A General Overview of the Qur'an

The Qur'an was revealed over a period of about 23 years. It began in 610, in the Hira Cave in the Mountain of Light (*Jabale Noor*). This is about two and a half miles away from the House of Allah in Mecca, Saudi Arabia. The first revelation is the first five verses of Sura 96 (S 96). This sura is called *Al-Alaq*:

"Read in the name of your Lord who created, created man from a clot. Read, for your Lord is most Generous, Who teaches by means of the pen, teaches man what he does not know." S 96:1-5

The last revelation is the third verse of Sura 5, which was "received" in 632:

"Today I perfected your religion for you and completed my favor to you and have chosen for you Al-Islam as your religion." S 5:3

The Qur'an is divided into thirty equal divisions which are called *juz*. In total, there are 114 chapters *(suras)*, of varying length. The chapters given before the migration of the Prophet to Medina are called *Makkan*. Those sent down after the migration are called *Madinan*. There is no logical sequence or arrangement in the text. The text includes laws, legends, prayers, curses, and modified stories of biblical characters. The 114 "chapters" of the Qur'an are called *suras* (or *surahs*) and each is given the name of a subject, person, group of people, or an event. To the Muslim the Qur'an is the source of all certainty. They never question it!

How did Muslims get the Qur'an?

There are four key words we must understand if we are to know how Muslims got the Qur'an. The key words are Revelation, Inspiration, Recitation, and Compilation. Let's look at each of the ways by which the Qur'an was developed. Whole books have been written about each of the following key words. We are looking at each briefly.

1. Muslim REVELATION

Muslims believe that the Qur'an is a new **revelation** from Allah. They believe that Allah did not speak directly to man. He supposedly spoke to the angel Gabriel, who gave the revelations to Mohammed. They believe the Qur'an is perfect. Muslims point to Surah 85:21-22 which says *'Nay this is a glorious Qur'an, (inscribed) in a tablet preserved."* These "revelations" were sent down (Surah 17:85) to the lowest of the seven heavens at the time of the month of Ramadan, during the night of power (*'Iailat al Qadr'*). From there the revelations were spoken to Mohammed through the angel Gabriel (Surah 25:32). They call the Qur'an the "Mother of Books" (Surah 43:3), and believe there is no other book or revelation which can compare. In fact, in both Surahs 2:23 and 10:37-38, man is challenged to "present some other book of equal beauty."

2. Muslim INSPIRATION

Muslims believe that the Qur'an is given by **inspiration.** The Arabic term which attempts to explain the process of revelation is the word "Wahy", which can mean "divine inspiration." In Surah 42:51 *Wahy* is explained: "It is not fitting for a man that Allah should speak to him except by inspiration, or from behind a veil, or by the sending of a Messenger to reveal, with Allah's permission, what Allah wills, for He is most high, most wise."

How did the inspiration happen? Muslim writers like Ibn Ishaq, Ibn Hisham, Ibn Athir, and 'Ali Halabi have written about Mohammed's experience. Their writings list seven ways Mohammed experienced *Wahy*.

- Mohammed would sweat vigorously when the revelations came, according to his wife Aisha. There was the sound of bells ringing in his ears. He would become greatly upset and his face would contort. 'Umar ibnu'l Khattab tells us that Mohammed would shiver, his mouth would foam, and he would roar like a camel.
- Wahy came to him in dreams while sleeping.
- At times, the inspiration would come while he was awake in visions.
- At times he saw an angel in the form of a tall young man.
- At other times he saw actual angels (S 42:51).
- During one evening (known as the *Mi'raj*) he was taken through the "Seven Heavens" to receive the revelation.
- Finally, Allah spoke to him from behind a veil (S 42:51).

3. Muslim RECITATION

Recitation is a most important concept about the Muslim scripture. Muslims believe that the Qur'an is a **"recitation"** of what Allah told Gabriel to tell Mohammed. Remember, the word q*ur'an* means "recitation." The Qur'an is made up of the verses that Mohammed recited while exhibiting behavior resembling seizures. His followers wrote the verses on any material that was at hand. Respect for the Qur'an grew after Mohammed's move to Medina. His followers believed that Mohammed was building on the Bible. They revered him as a prophet equal to Abraham and Moses.

Recitations Were Memorized

Mohammed's recitations or sayings were written on dried leaves, bleached bones, stones and other available materials. No one volume was available during his lifetime. Only scattered fragments existed when Mohammed died. These fragments were kept in several places. Abu Bakr (Mohammed's successor), Umar, and Fatima (Mohammed's daughter) each had collections of these fragments. Most of the recitations were preserved by "memorizers" called *Hafiz*. At that time, most Islamic teaching was passed on verbally.

Recitations Were Preserved in Writing

Many early Muslims lost their lives in the battles for the spread of the religion. Some who had memorized the passages were killed. This meant that parts of Allah's revelations were being lost. The words of the Muslim god were being lost! Recognizing the problem, Abu Bakr commissioned a codifying (writing down) of the messages that had been memorized or written on scattered materials. All was collected and the collection was passed on to the succeeding Muslim leaders called *caliphs*.

Collecting the recitations did not solve all problems. Instead, it created a dilemma. For several reasons, Muslim leaders began to debate over the collection.

- No one had access to the original and official text.
- Very few could even quote the official text.
- As recitations had been written down, the language was often vague and led to different interpretations.

Muslim leaders began to see the danger of having a diversity of texts that allowed for different interpretations.

4. Muslim COMPILATION

How was the Qur'an compiled? As stated, Muslims believe that the Qur'an is the final revelation from Allah dictated and recited through Gabriel to Mohammed. He in turn recited it to others who memorized or wrote down the recitation on whatever was available. Some say that the shoulder blade of a camel was used at least once. These written revelations were edited and complied into the Qur'an after Mohammed's death in 632 AD.

It is important to keep in mind that the Qur'an is written in Arabic. Arabic was Mohammed's native tongue. Muslim purists do not see an English translation or any translation from the original Arabic as authoritative. This is a problem in that a large number of Muslims do not read or speak Arabic. The average Muslim must go to trained Islamic spiritual leaders to find out what their scripture teaches. This arrangement puts a tremendous amount of power in the hands of Islamic experts like *imams*. Muslims can hide behind this "screen" and say that non-Arabic speakers do not fully understand the Qur'an. One writer says,

> "The means by which revelation was given was the language (Arabic), not Mohammed. The central role of the language means that what God has said is inseparable from the way (through a particular language) the thoughts were expressed. So the meaning of the Qur'an cannot be conveyed exactly in any words other than the original Arabic words of the book." (*The Cross and the Crescent*, Alpharetta, GA: North Am. Mission Board, SBC)

An Official Version of the Qur'an Formed

The need for an official authoritative text became clear. There would be no harmony or unity among followers of Islam without it. Zayd, an aide to Mohammed, was appointed by Caliph Uthman to assemble all available texts and dictate them to scribes in order to produce an official and authoritative copy of Mohammed's recitations. This became the *Qur'an*. Four copies were issued and kept in strategic places like Medina and Damascus. It is important to note that all *other texts were destroyed.*

Even the new text did not eliminate all difficulties. Many words in the text had double meanings that allowed much to be read into the text. Errors in reading and pronunciation were not easy to resolve. At the time of the writing there was no standardized form of grammar to help with these important details. Eventually seven different readings of the Qur'an became possible. Later that number was reduced to two.

When we think of how the Qur'an was compiled, or put together, it brings up several important questions:

- How did Zayd know what to include and exclude from the official collection? It appears that one man made some very significant decisions at this point in the history of the Qur'an.
- Who decided what an "unofficial" text was?
- How do we know if the Qur'an of today is not in conflict with older manuscripts from the time of Mohammed?

Muslims usually answer those questions by saying that Allah is powerful enough to preserve his texts through the ages. Really? We must think through that for a moment and apply it to Jesus. Muslims agree that Jesus was a prophet. If He was a prophet, why was Allah not powerful enough to preserve Jesus' words as recorded in the Bible? Yet, Muslims say the Bible has been corrupted, not preserved.

Muslim Core Beliefs about the Qur'an

- Every word of the Qur'an is supposedly from the mouth of Allah.
- It should be placed on the highest shelf of your home with nothing on top of it.
- You must do *wudu* (ceremonial cleansing) before you touch the Qur'an. After reading, you close it, kiss it, and touch it to your forehead.

- Muslims believe it is perfect only in the Arabic language (Allah's language). All Muslims worldwide must read the Qur'an in Arabic.

Since not all Muslims know Arabic, only about 20% understand what they are reading. Translations are considered inferior by Muslim scholars. Logically, this means only 20% of Muslims worldwide are true, devout, Qur'an-reading Muslims.

In general, the Qur'an is seen as the completion (final correction) of the Bible. Muslims believe that Jews had the true word, but corrupted it because they added an emphasis on the "messiah." Muslims reject the idea of a messiah. Muslims also believe that the Christians had the true word, but corrupted it with the changes made in the Gospels by Paul and the Apostles. The Qur'an claims to reveal hidden details to astound mankind. For example, the Qur'an announced that nineteen angels guard Hell (Sura 74:26-31). This news was expected to amaze the Christians into believing in the Qur'an.

Lambs, Foxes, and Lions

Some passages of the Qur'an were given while Mohammed was just getting started. At first, he was in the minority. Passages 'received' during this time are those that promote peace with other faiths. After all, in a start-up religion you would want the existing religions of the time to tolerate and accept that you have something new from God. This would be the time to appear as meek and mild, like a lamb. Moderate and secular Muslims refer to passages written during this "lamb" time to teach that Islam is a religion that promotes tolerance and peace. But that is not the end of the story.

Soon Mohammed became a theo-political leader of a large following. As his followers grew he did not have to worry as much about the other pagan religions of his day. This would have been a time to be sly or wise as a fox. We must admit that not much is written about a time when Mohammed faced equals and competed in the arena of ideas on a level playing field. Instead, he eliminated opposition mercilessly. Islam's invasion of the West in the 20th Century might be seen as a time of being wise or "sly as a fox."

As time went by Mohammed enjoyed political and military victories, such as capturing the city of Mecca. Mohammed became the leader of the majority. As the leader of the majority he now could be bold as a lion. During this "lion" stage his recitations say things that amount to "kill the infidel!" Passages written during this time are the ones that the extremists of today quote.

More Muslim Beliefs about the Qur'an

The following beliefs may or may not be core beliefs of every Muslim. Nevertheless, my Muslim friends hold dearly to them!

- The Qur'an is a revelation from Allah, who is the lord of the worlds, the mighty, and the wise.
- The Qur'an was revealed to Mohammed because he was the final prophet.
- The Qur'an claims to confirm the books of the former prophets and to complete them. Mohammed is the final prophet.
- Abraham is said to have been a Muslim, and his son Ishmael founded the Arab race; therefore, Mohammed, an Arab, is in the prophetic line.
- The Holy Spirit revealed it to Mohammed. Some Muslim commentators say the Holy Spirit is the angel Gabriel who is said to have brought the revelations from heaven to Mohammed.
- It was brought down from the highest to the lowest heaven on the "Night of Majesty" about the 27th day of the month of Ramadan. Muslims call this night *"Lailat al-Qadr"* or literally, "night of majesty, grandeur, greatness or power." Gabriel is said to have revealed the first part of the Qur'an to Mohammed on this night.
- The Qur'an is eternal and uncreated, having existed in heaven from the beginning of time. It was revealed to Mohammed at the appointed time. It is to be read and believed.
- The Qur'an is a miracle of God. When Mohammed was challenged to produce a miracle to prove his apostleship he

pointed to a chapter of the Qur'an demanding that his opponents produce one like it.
- The Qur'an was originally revealed in Arabic because Arabic is the language of heaven.

> From this we see an argument that Muslims raise. They say that whereas we have to translate our Bible from Hebrew and Greek causing inevitable differences, the Qur'an came in Arabic. Some Muslim teachers therefore say that the Qur'an is untranslatable.

- The pages of the Qur'an are pure and its directions are right.

A Personal Note

Muslims show great respect for their holy book. While I was a young, shave-head US Marine (Infantry), my first roommate was a Muslim. His name was Abdul Mohammed. We were stationed on Guam in 1982. We lived in close quarters and I saw his respect for his holy book. He always put it on the top shelf in his locker and never placed anything on top of it. I did the same to show respect for my Bible. We were both about 19 years old and we were both firmly committed to our belief systems. As you might suspect, we had some heated discussions. How I wish I could go back and have those discussions with him again!

Twenty five years later, my family and I invited some international students from the local university to attend church with us. Two Muslim friends from Kashmir joined us for services. My 17 year old son, Daniel, was sitting next to Ali. Daniel had his legs crossed in a manly fashion and was resting his Bible on the crossed leg. Ali noticed that the Bible was slightly touching Daniel's shoe. Instinctively he reached over and moved the Bible so it would not touch Daniel's shoe. We are sure he did it out of respect for what he perceives to be a holy book. Showing greater respect for Scripture might be a small lesson we Christians can learn from Muslim friends.

Muslim Qur'an Summarized

Muslims see the Qur'an as the inspired, revealed, authoritative, perfect word of God (Allah–not Jehovah) given through Mohammed, a man who was selected to be the prophet.

Bible believers disagree!!

The Mormon "Quad"

While on active duty as a Marine, my first roommate was a Muslim. My last roommate was a Mormon. My Mormon friend and I had many friendly discussions about religion. I wish I could go back and have them again now. A Calvinist might say I was predestined to write about Muslim and Mormon belief because God graciously gave me a roommate from each religion. Since I am a Calvinist of some degree, I agree!

"Quad" is a nickname not officially endorsed by the Latter-day Saints. I heard it first from my Mormon roommate. An internet search using "Mormon Quad" will bring up numerous hits and show that many Mormons use the term.

Incidentally, it is worth noting that back in 1984, my Mormon roommate did not want to be called Christian. He preferred to be called "LDS" (Latter-day Saint). However, Mormon folk today wish to be called Christians. In fact, in a recent dialogue with two Mormon missionaries I asked them specifically if they refer to themselves as Christians. Their response was an emphatic "Yes!" I have a pastor friend now serving in Utah who is appalled that Mormons are teaching their kids to sing the "I am a C, I am a C-H, I am a C-H-R-I-S-T-I-A-N" song. Obviously, they are trying to identify with mainline historic Christianity.

Why use this nickname? The value of using *"Quad"* is that it will help us remember that Mormon folk have four separate books. These books are distinctly different as we shall see.

The Mormon Quad is actually four books bound together. It is made up of a *KJV Bible, The Book of Mormon, Pearl of Great Price*, and *Doctrine and Covenants*. These are the General Works that provide the basis for Mormonism. They are the Mormon scriptures. Let me offer a brief description of each.

KJV (King James Version) Bible

Wow! Who can offer a simple, brief description of this English Bible? The KJV Bible is the greatest piece of English literature ever printed. It has reigned supreme as the predominate English translation of the Word of God for almost 400 years. I own a page from a 1688-90 KJV Bible. Each time I look at it I find it incredible to think of the millions who have read that superb English translation and received the wonderful free gift of salvation in Christ! The KJV is a great, reliable, literal English translation of the Word of God. For our purpose here, let me make just a few points that relate to Mormonism and the KJV.

- The KJV was probably what Joseph Smith "cut his teeth on." Historians describe Joseph as barely literate. If he had gone to school at all he would have been exposed to this Bible. It was by far the most common English version of the Bible at that time. Unlike today, the Bible was a common textbook in the education system of the early 1800's. It is no surprise that he referenced it and even plagiarized from it.
- Mormon folk say they believe the Bible "so far as it is properly translated."
- A main purpose for the 1611 translation, financed by King James of England, was to get the Word of God into the language of the common man. The English usage in the KJV is the way men talked on the street back then. It could be that Mormon folk endorse the KJV (and no other version) because "King James English" does not communicate to the common man as well today as it did in the 17th and 18th century. That "cloudy" communication makes the other books more easily understood and actually draws the reader to them instead of the Bible.

In short, Mormons give lip service to the Bible by including it in the Quad. But, when their books disagree with the Bible, they give priority to their own books.

Book of Mormon

The second book in the Quad is the Book of Mormon. What is this book? Let's start this way.

A long, long time ago, in a place far, far away there were a people who were in danger of being destroyed. There was an evil empire that wanted to crush them. So they were given some special instructions that warned them of coming destruction. They had to flee from their land. They took off in their ships toward a strange new world. They brought their advanced weapons and knowledge with them and settled into the new place.

Soon they were fighting among themselves. The people polarized into a dark skinned group and a light skinned group. They fought an epic war. Finally, the dark skinned group completely destroyed the light skinned group in a great battle where tens of thousands, at least, were slaughtered.

Does that sound fanciful? Like Star Wars?

Mormons actually believe a story like that. It is the Book of Mormon story. It is both futuristic and ancient at the same time. To Mormons, the story of the Book of Mormon is not a fable. They consider it factual history!

The Book of Mormon is purported to be a history of Jewish people who were directed by God to leave the Middle East and come to the Western Hemisphere. Supposedly around the time of the Tower of Babel, the Jaredites (led by Jared) were told to leave. Again in about 600 BC (NOTE: BC not AD) a man named Lehi was instructed by God to take his family and come to the new world (North America). Two of Lehi's sons became the leaders of great peoples. Nephi, the youngest son, produced the Nephites who were light skinned people. Laman, the eldest, produced the Lamanites who were dark skinned people. They fought and the Lamanites won by killing all the Nephites. So there you have it. That is the Book of Mormon in one paragraph!

The name "Mormon" comes from a pivotal man in Joseph Smith's "history." It is not taken from archeological finds or from any accepted history written by a non-Mormon. According to Joseph, Mormon was the father of Moroni. Joseph taught that, in the 400's AD, Mormon wrote down the history of his people including a story of Jesus appearing to people in the Western Hemisphere. Mormon's son, Moroni, edited what Mormon wrote and it ended up on plates of gold. Moroni hid the plates in a stone box and they remained hidden until the 1820's.

Somehow the man Moroni, became a "resurrected being" that we know as the Angel Moroni. Mormons offer no account for how this man became an angel. The now Angel Moroni came to Joseph Smith so that he could instruct him as to where to find the gold plates. Joseph would translate the information from the plates. The "translation" of the gold plates is named after the father. We know it as the Book of Mormon.

Why Publish the Book of Mormon?

First, this is supposed to be God's revelation by Joseph Smith. Joseph was confused by the religious systems (Baptist, Methodist, Presbyterian, Congregationalist, etc.) of his day. He went into the woods to pray for understanding, and had a supernatural encounter with Moroni. According to Joseph, Moroni told him where to find the plates of gold. He found them but had to translate them from a supposed language called *Reformed Egyptian Hieroglyphics*. There are conflicting accounts about how Joseph actually accomplished the translation of the plates into the Book of Mormon. But, Mormons today say that the Book of Mormon is as important and as authoritative as the Bible. Even more, they say that it is the truest book ever written.

There were also some very practical reasons for Joseph to publish such a book. We need to remember that Joseph Smith lived in America in the early 1800's. America was growing and trying to find her place in the world. Joseph's Book of Mormon provided a very convenient justification for the discriminatory social situation of his day. The Book of Mormon could be viewed as God's "explanation" of why there were dark skinned people (Native Americans) in the new world when Columbus arrived later in 1492. This "history" could also explain why there are ruins of great civilizations (Inca and Mayan) in the Americas.

Conveniently, the book also points to the supposed superiority of the light skinned races. This would make the cruel treatment of Native Americans and African slaves more justifiable. The Lamanites, dark skinned, are portrayed as an evil, truth-rejecting race that viciously and selfishly destroyed the light skinned race. In Joseph's day, this would have made white people feel better about enslaving blacks and killing Indians. At that time people could say, "After all, they deserve it because their ancestors were evil." The Book of Mormon was a perfect match for American culture of the early 1800's.

What's the Big Deal?

So what's the big deal about a far-fetched ancient history? The danger is not in the history, although there are plenty of good reasons for rejecting it as a legitimate history. Those reasons range from archaeology to DNA. For example, the Book of Mormon contains many plagiarisms of the King James Bible (at least 25,000 words). This is strange since the plates were supposed to have been in the ground many centuries before the King James Bible was completed in 1611! The Book of Mormon also contains many errors such as claims of elephants and horses in the Western Hemisphere and advanced metal producing capabilities in America before 400 AD.

**The real danger does not lie in the content of the Book of Mormon!
The real danger is in accepting what the Book of Mormon does to Joseph Smith!**

When you accept the Book of Mormon as inspired, you elevate Joseph Smith from a treasure hunter and crystal ball mystic into

God's spokesman. A person can read the Book of Mormon and say, "Yeah, I can accept it. I can't prove it or disprove it but I will accept it." Doing that is dangerous because it makes Joseph Smith an authoritative prophet! You have agreed that he speaks for God! The problem is that other things he spoke and taught as truth are far more damnable than a questionable ancient history.

The Book of Mormon is like a doorway. The door itself is neutral. It is neither good nor bad. However, Mormons make a big deal of accepting it as "Another Testament of Jesus Christ." They want hearers to accept the Book of Mormon as more of God's word given through Joseph Smith. Once a person accepts that Joseph is a direct channel from God, you enter a dangerous situation. Like the movie characters Qui-Gon and Obe-Wan, the person who accepts the Book of Mormon steps thru the doorway into a "room" that quickly fills with the poisonous gas of Mormon teachings.

Mormons want converts to step through the door into "Joseph." They see accepting the Book of Mormon as crucial! At one time Lavar Thornock was head of the religion department of Brigham Young University. Concerning the Book of Mormon, he wrote:

> "No one could possibly be saved and reject it. . . if false, no one could possibly be saved and accept it."

Their absolute insistence on accepting the Book of Mormon is based on their need to see Joseph as God's prophet. Mormonism rises or falls on Joseph Smith's credibility.

We have looked at the first two books of the Mormon Quad. Let's move to the last two. They are *Doctrine and Covenants* and *Pearl of Great Price*. This is where the heresy begins in earnest!

Doctrine and Covenants

The third book is *Doctrine and Covenants* (abbreviated "D&C"). What is D&C? The introductory section of the General Works tells us. This is how the Mormon Church speaks:

"The *Doctrine and Covenants* is a collection of divine revelations and inspired declarations given for the establishment and regulation of the kingdom of God on the earth in the last days. Although most of the sections are directed to members of The Church of Jesus Christ of Latter-day Saints, the messages, warnings, and exhortations are for the benefit of all mankind, and contain an invitation to all people everywhere to hear the voice of the Lord Jesus Christ, speaking to them for their temporal well-being and their everlasting salvation.

"Most of the revelations in this compilation were received through Joseph Smith, Jr.,[1] the first prophet and president of The Church of Jesus Christ of Latter-day Saints. Others were issued through some of his successors in the Presidency.

"The book of Doctrine and Covenants is one of the standard works of the Church in company with the Holy Bible, the Book of Mormon, and the Pearl of Great Price. However, the Doctrine and Covenants is unique because it is not a translation of an ancient document, but is of modern origin and was given of God through his chosen prophets for the restoration of his holy work and the establishment of the kingdom of God on the earth in these days. In the revelations one hears the tender but firm voice of the Lord Jesus Christ, speaking anew in the dispensation of the fullness of times; and the work that is initiated herein is preparatory to his second coming, in fulfillment of and in concert with the words of all the holy prophets since the world began."

Mormons see the D& C as authoritative because it comes through Joseph. A basic for Christians to remember is that Mormon folk have accepted Joseph Smith as God's prophet, channel, and spokesperson. Their view is that when he declares, "Thus saith the Lord," his words are as authoritative and binding as the New and Old Testaments.

This is dangerous in that it opens the door for new doctrines. Polygamy is an example of a new doctrine that the D&C endorses and justifies while The Book of Mormon clearly forbids it.

- Doctrine and Covenants endorses polygamy.

  ". . .if any man espouse a virgin, and desire to espouse another, and the first give her consent, and *if he espouse the second, and they are virgins, and have vowed to no other man, then he is justified; he cannot commit adultery.* . .And if he have ten virgins given unto him by this law, he cannot commit adultery." (Doctrine and Covenants, 132:61, 62)

- The Book of Mormon expressly forbids polygamy.

  "24 Behold, David and Solomon truly had many wives and concubines, which thing was abominable before me, saith the Lord. . .Wherefore, my brethren, hear me, and hearken to the word of the Lord*: For there shall not any man among you have save it be one wife; and concubines he shall have none; 28 For I, the Lord God, delight in the chastity of women.* And whoredoms are an abomination before me; thus saith the Lord of Hosts."(Book of Mormon, Jacob 2:24-28)

Mormons also cite the D&C to back their claim to be the only true church. Mormon Apostle, Bruce R. McConkie emphatically declared this truth as part of Mormon Doctrine. He cites D&C in the following quote.

"This Church is *'the only true and living church* upon the face of the whole earth' (D&C 1:30), the *only organization* authorized by the Almighty to preach his gospel and administer the ordinances of salvation, *the only Church* which has power to save and exalt men in the hereafter. . .. There *is no salvation outside this one true church,* the Church of Jesus Christ." (*Mormon Doctrine*, 1979, pp. 136,138)

Pearl of Great Price

The last book that is bound together in the Mormon Quad is called *Pearl of Great Price*. Again, let's go straight to a Mormon source to see how they describe it. The quote below is taken from the introduction section of the *General Works* (Quad).

"The Pearl of Great Price is a selection of choice materials touching many significant aspects of the faith and doctrine of The Church of Jesus Christ of Latter-day Saints. These items were produced by the Prophet Joseph Smith and were published in the Church periodicals of his day.

"The first collection of materials carrying the title Pearl of Great Price was made in 1851 by Elder Franklin D. Richards, then a member of the Council of the Twelve and president of the British Mission. Its purpose was to make more readily accessible some important articles that had had limited circulation in the time of Joseph Smith. As Church membership increased throughout Europe and America there was a need to make these items available. The Pearl of Great Price received wide use and subsequently became a standard work of the Church by action of the First Presidency and the general conference in Salt Lake City on October 10, 1880.

"Several revisions have been made in the contents as the needs of the Church have required. In 1878 portions of the Book of Moses not contained in the first edition were added. In 1902 certain parts of the Pearl of Great Price that duplicated material also published in the Doctrine and Covenants were omitted. Arrangement into chapters and verses, with footnotes, was done in 1902. The first publication in double-column pages, with index, was in 1921. No other changes were made until April 1976, when two items of revelation were added. In 1979 these two items were removed from the Pearl of Great Price and placed in the Doctrine and Covenants, where they now appear as Sections 137 and 138. In the present edition some changes have been made to bring the text into conformity with earlier documents."

The most important feature of Pearl of Great Price is that it tells the official story of Joseph Smith becoming God's spokesman. This is the Mormon story of the First Vision.

"So, in accordance with this, my determination to ask of God, I retired to the woods to make the attempt. It was on the morning of a beautiful, clear day, early in the spring of eighteen hundred and twenty. It was the first time in my life that I had made such an attempt, for amidst all my anxieties I had never as yet made the attempt to pray vocally.

15 After I had retired to the place where I had previously designed to go, having looked around me, and finding myself alone, I kneeled down and began to offer up the desires of my heart to God. I had scarcely done so, when immediately I was seized upon by some power which entirely overcame me, and had such an astonishing influence over me as to bind my tongue so that I could not speak. Thick darkness gathered around me, and it seemed to me for a time as if I were doomed to sudden destruction.

16 But, exerting all my powers to call upon God to deliver me out of the power of this enemy which had seized upon me, and at the very moment when I was ready to sink into despair and abandon myself to destruction—not to an imaginary ruin, but to the power of some actual being from the unseen world, who had such marvelous power as I had never before felt in any being—just at this moment of great alarm, I saw a pillar of light exactly over my head, above the brightness of the sun, which descended gradually until it fell upon me.

17 It no sooner appeared than I found myself delivered from the enemy which held me bound. When the light rested upon me I saw two Personages, whose brightness and glory defying all description, standing above me in the air. One of them spake unto me, calling me by name and said, pointing to the other—This is My Beloved Son. Hear Him!

18 My object in going to inquire of the Lord was to know which of all the sects was right, that I might know which to join. No sooner, therefore, did I get possession of myself, so as to be able to speak, than I asked the Personages who stood above me in the light, which of all the sects was right (for

at this time it had never entered into my heart that all were wrong)—and which I should join.

19 I was answered that I must join none of them, for they were all wrong; and the Personage who addressed me said that all their creeds were an abomination in his sight; that those professors were all corrupt; that: "they draw near to me with their lips, but their hearts are far from me, they teach for doctrines the commandments of men, having a form of godliness, but they deny the power thereof"

20 He again forbade me to join with any of them; and many other things did he say unto me, which I cannot write at this time. When I came to myself again, I found myself lying on my back, looking up into heaven. When the light had departed, I had no strength; but soon recovering in some degree, I went home." (The First Vision: Pearl of Great Price, Joseph Smith – History- Ch 1 vv 14-20)

Mormons look to this First Vision story in Pearl of Great Price as a verification of Joseph Smith as a prophet of God.

The Mormon Quad Summarized

Mormons see the Quad as the inspired, revealed, authoritative, perfect word of God given through Joseph Smith, Jr., a man who was selected to be the prophet.

Bible believers disagree!!

The Word of God

What do Christians Believe about Scripture?

Evangelical Christians believe that the Bible is the inspired, inerrant Word of God to man. Note the remarkable similarities of the next two paragraphs.

- Evangelical Christians believe that when Mohammed received his revelations from the angel, he should have filtered all the new material through the Bible! Mohammed did not square his recitation with the Bible, so there are some significant, eternal differences between his recitations and the revealed Word of God.

• Likewise, we Evangelical Christians believe that when Joseph Smith had a supernatural encounter with beings who supposedly gave him new revelation, he should have filtered all the new material through the Bible! Joseph Smith did not square his revelations with the Bible, so there are some significant, eternal differences between his revelations and the legitimate Word of God.

Basics of the Christian View of Scripture

Mormons and Muslims are taught not to question the origins of their scriptures. On the other hand, Christians are always encouraged to be serious students of how the Bible came to man. Truth loves light and loves to be examined.

This last section will deal with some fundamental ideas that Christians should understand and to be able to defend. Entire books have been written about each of the following ideas. The reader is encouraged to study beyond the next few pages. Use them as a springboard for your own investigation into the reliability of the Bible.

Revelation

We believe that God has revealed Himself in nature, history, and conscience. We believe that He has also revealed Himself in His Son and in His Word. When we use the word "revelation" as it pertains to the Bible, we are referring to God directly (not indirectly) revealing things about Himself that He wants recorded in written form. Revelation is the communication or unveiling of truth. God must do the revealing.

Revelation is not Inspiration

Inspiration concerns recording or writing down the revealed truth. It is possible to have revelation without inspiration. One clear example of revelation without inspiration is in Revelation 10:3. In this passage John heard the seven thunders utter their voices but was not permitted to write what they said.

On the other hand we may also have inspiration without direct revelation. Luke is the primary example of this idea. He wrote what he had seen with his own eyes as well as what he discovered by research (Luke 1:1-4). All of what he wrote was, and is, inspired of God. Luke, as a historian, searched out written records and verified oral tradition in the penning of his gospel. He was also an eyewitness to much of Acts. Conversely the Apostle John received much of the Book of Revelation directly from God. Both men were inspired in the writing of their material, but the material was received in different ways. Of course, in the broader sense, we speak of the whole of Scripture as God's self-revelation. Sometimes His self-revelation came directly. At other times it came indirectly, through God's involvement in human history.

Inspiration

Inspiration has to do with the recording of truth in writing. The Spirit of God moved upon men to write each of the sixty-six books of the Bible. The New Testament book of II Peter 1:21says:

"...for no prophecy was ever made by an act of human will, but men moved by the Holy Spirit spoke from God."

Scripture is fully and verbally inspired. In the same way that breath forms words, God breathed His Word both *to* man and *for* man.

"All Scripture is inspired by God and profitable for teaching, for reproof, for correction, for training in righteousness; so that the man of God may be adequate, equipped for every good work." 2 Timothy 3:16

A Definition of Inspiration

A proper definition must be scriptural. The bare-bones definition is that God "carried men along" so that they wrote His message as the Bible. Putting some meat on those bones leads to a definition like this:

> "My own definition of biblical inspiration is that it is God's superintendence of the human authors so that, using their own individual personalities, they composed and recorded without error His revelation to man in the words of the original autographs." (Charles Ryrie, *Ryrie Study Bible* (Expanded Edition) KJV, Moody Press, 1986, p. 1985.)

Notice important words in that definition.

- The word "superintendence" allows for a broad range of relationships God had with both the writers and the great variety of writing. His superintendence was sometimes very direct. At other times it was more indirect. However it always included guarding the writers so that they wrote accurately.
- The word "composed" shows that the writers were not always simply passive stenographers to whom God dictated the material. It shows that some were active writers who allowed God to use their intellect.
- "Without error" expresses the Bible's own claim to be truth.

"Sanctify them in the truth; Your word is truth." John 17:17

- Inspiration applies only to the "original writings." It does not apply to copies or translations, however accurate they may be.

We should never lose sight of the incredible claims the Bible makes for itself in this matter of inspiration. No other book can compare with it. God breathed it. God controlled the men who wrote it. We are blessed to possess it.

Authority

The Bible carries with it the divine authority of God. It is binding upon man: on his mind, conscience, will, and heart. Man, creed, and church are all subject to the authority of Scripture. God has spoken; we must submit. The eternal "thus saith the Lord" is our standard.

Inerrancy

Not only is Scripture inspired and authoritative, it is also inerrant and infallible. By this we mean that it is without error in the original manuscripts. It is inerrant in all that it affirms, whether in historical, scientific, moral, or doctrinal matters. Inerrancy extends to all of Scripture and is not limited to certain teachings of Scripture.

Illumination

To illuminate something is to light it up, to make it clear, and to explain it. We believe that the Lord "shines light" into the darkness of men's minds as they interact with His Word. The One who inspired men in the writing of Scripture also illumines the minds of those who read it. The Bible teaches that because of sin and the darkened understanding sin caused, without God's help no one can understand Scripture properly.

> "For even though they knew God, they did not honor Him as God or give thanks, but they became futile in their speculations, and their foolish heart was darkened." Romans 1:21
> "...being darkened in their understanding, excluded from the life of God because of the ignorance that is in them, because of the hardness of their heart..." Ephesians 4:18

God the Spirit enlightens the mind of the believer to understand the Scriptures. This is not the same as inspiration because it focuses on understanding what has already been written. Inspiration and Illumination are not the same. Inspiration focuses on **writing** it down without error. Illumination focuses on **understanding** what is written.

The Bible is ALL of God's Word!

We believe that the Bible is all there is! We believe that God is finished revealing His written words to man. Christians should not look for more books from God. Why do we believe this? It's what the Bible teaches.

There are several passages of Scripture that build a case for what theologians call the "closing of the canon." The strongest argument that supports this position is found in the last book of the Bible, the book of Revelation. The Bible gives us this key teaching concerning whether or not there will be more books.

> "I testify to everyone who hears the words of the prophecy of this book, if anyone adds to them, God will add to him the plagues which are written in this book; and if anyone takes away from the words of the book of this prophecy, God will take away his part from the tree to life and from the Holy City, which are written in this book." Revelation 22:18-19

Some apply these verses only to the book of Revelation and say they do not close the door on other books like the Qur'an and the Book of Mormon. There are several reasons to reject this interpretation and to say that they close the door on the whole written revelation from God. Here are the reasons.

- Revelation is the perfect "finish line." Genesis, the first book of the Bible, moves us from eternity to the start of time. Revelation, the last book of the Bible, paints a detailed picture of future events that lead from time into eternity. Like the start and finish lines of a drag strip, Genesis and Revelation are perfectly matched lines of transition from and to eternity.
- John is the perfect finishing author. The Apostle John met all the qualifications as an authorized prophet and apostle. No man alive can verify claims to being authorized like John. When John finished writing and warned against future writing we do well to agree and say that it is done.
- This warning passage of Revelation 22 promises the severest consequences if disobeyed. This is a unique warning that

comes about 20 years after other New Testament books were finished. This points to a unique END.

• Those who lived in John's day gave record that they believed this was the close of God's written Revelation.

Chapter Conclusion

Bible Christians reject the Qur'an and the Quad as holy books.

We do not believe that they are inspired by God. We believe that they contain ideas that do not agree with what the Bible clearly teaches. We believe that they each also serve to elevate a single man to the highest office of "spokesman for God."

Chapter 3

Questions for Discussion

1. Should Christians spend time reading and studying the holy books of other faiths?
2. What are the holy books of other Cults? Other Religions?
3. How do other religions show respect for writings they consider holy?
4. Is there anything (horoscopes, proverbs, etc.) that you consider equal to the Bible?
5. Are you able to defend your faith using Scripture? How could you improve this?

.

Chapter 4

Lifting Their Fathers' Fingerprints

❖❖❖

Is God the Father a Bad Dad?

T his chapter seeks to find out whether Allah or Elohim is the same
God who is revealed in the Holy Bible. This is a crucial either/or
question. When asked, Muslims and Mormons alike quickly answer,
"Yes! He is the same! The scripture declares it!" The implication is
that we Christians should believe it because the scripture says so. A
better way to know is to look at the evidence. We need to investigate
the nature and attributes of Allah as presented in their source documents, and compare them with the biblical God–Jehovah/Yahweh.

What Kind of Dad is "Father" Allah?

We will first examine how the Qur'an describes Allah. Then we
will compare that to how the Bible describes Yahweh.

Allah can be a schemer or deceiver.

> "Verily, the hypocrites *seek to deceive* Allah, *but it is
> He Who deceives them.* And when they stand up for As-
> Salat (the prayer), they stand with laziness and to be seen
> of men, and they do not remember Allah but little." S. 4:142
> Hilali-Khan

"And (the unbelievers) *schemed* and planned, and Allah *schemed also, and the best of schemers is Allah.*" S. 3:54

"Are they then secure from *Allah's scheme (makra Allahi)*? None deemeth himself secure from *Allah's scheme (makra Allahi)* save folk that perish." S. 7:99 Pickthall

"Remember how the unbelievers *schemed* against thee, to keep thee in bonds, or to slay thee, or get thee out (of thy home). They *scheme* and plot, *but the best of schemers is Allah.*" S. 8:30

"And when We (Allah) make people taste of mercy after an affliction touches them, lo! *They devise schemes (makrun)* against our communication. Say: *Allah is quicker to scheme (makran)*; surely our apostles write down what you plan." S. 10:21

"And those before them did indeed scheme (makara), *but all scheming (al-makru) is Allah's*; He knows what every soul earns, and the unbelievers shall come to know for whom is the (better) issue of the abode." S. 13:42

"So *they schemed a scheme*: and *We schemed a scheme*, while they perceived not." S. 27:50

When we look at these verses from the Qur'an it is important that we study a specific Arabic word that is used. The Arabic term for "scheme" is *makara* which refers to "one who is a deceiver, one who is conniving, and a schemer." The key is understanding that this word is <u>always</u> used in a negative sense. Therefore the picture of Allah that the Qur'an paints is that Allah is the best of deceivers, the premiere schemer and conniving one.

A Muslim might answer, "That is a Christian definition of the word." A Christian could then respond by pointing out that non-Christian Arabic speaking persons use this definition of *makara* (deceiver, schemer, conniving one). It is <u>not</u> only a Christian interpretation. It is the perspective of Muslim theologians as well. One example is Dr. Mahmoud M. Ayoub. He even brings up the question of how the word *makr* (scheming or plotting), which implies deceitfulness or dishonesty, could be attributed to God. [1]

The Qur'an gives examples of Allah devising evil:

"Remember in thy dream Allah showed them as a few: *if he had showed them to thee as many, ye would surely have been discouraged, and ye would surely have disputed in your decision:* but Allah saved you: for He knoweth well the (secrets) of (all) hearts." S. 8:43

A plain interpretation of this is that Allah caused Mohammed to see forces fighting against him as only a few. If he had shown them as they actually were, the Muslims would have been afraid to fight. This means that Allah had to use deception about the strength of the enemy in order to encourage the Muslims to fight for him.

Here is another quote from the Qur'an.

"They (*Jinns*–demon spirits) worked for him (Solomon) as he desired . . . then when we decreed death upon him, nothing showed them his death except a little creeping creature of the earth, which gnawed away at his staff. And when he fell the Jinns saw clearly how, *if they had known the unseen, they would not have continued in the humiliating penalty (of work)."* S. 34:13-14

The interpretation is that Allah deceived the Jinns. Allah wanted them to continue their work. Evidently if they had known of Solomon's death, they would have stopped their *"humiliating penalty of work."* The point is that Allah deceived them by preventing them from knowing of Solomon's death.

Allah's deception is also directed toward Christians and Jews. Allah deceived both Christians and Jews into thinking that Jesus was crucified when in fact "it was so made to appear unto them," seeing that he never was crucified or killed. S. 4:157

In contrast, the Bible teaches that Yahweh cannot lie. Titus 1:2 states plainly that God "cannot lie." Also, He does not tempt men to do evil. Evil is immorality and sin – or anything contrary to God's holy character. The Bible says:

"Let no one say when he is tempted, "I am being tempted by God"; for God cannot be tempted by evil, and He Himself does not tempt anyone." James 1:13

"Your eyes are too pure to approve evil. And You can not look on wickedness with favor." Habakkuk 1:13

A Muslim might be referring to the notion that Jeremiah had been deceived by God in Jeremiah 20:7.

"O LORD, thou hast deceived me and I was deceived." (KJV)

These objections can be answered easily by understanding the terms used in both passages. In 2 Sam. 17:14, the word translated as evil (KJV) is the Hebrew *ra*. Accordingly, some Hebrew scholars see it as being derived from the word *ra'a* which means to "break, smash, crush." The word *ra'a* can also be translated as adversity, affliction, calamity, distress, evil, or grief. The point of the passage is that God was bringing a calamity or a "crushing" upon Absalom because of Absalom's sin.

The other Bible passage mentioned is Jeremiah 20:7. In this passage the Hebrew term *pathath* is translated as "deceive." This word can also be translated as allure, enlarge, entice, deceive, flatter, or persuade. Since any one of the words can be used for *pathath,* we need to look at the context to see which is best. In such situations it is from the context we get the best meaning.

The context shows that the best translation is "persuade." Jeremiah is complaining that God is persuading him to continue his ministry, even though he wants to quit his service for God. This is one of those cases where a translation other than the KJV makes the theology clearer:

"O LORD, You induced me, and I was *persuaded;* You are stronger than I, and have prevailed. I am in derision daily; everyone mocks me. For when I spoke, I cried out; I shouted, 'Violence and plunder!' Because the word of the LORD was made to me a reproach and a derision daily. Then I said, 'I will not make mention of Him, nor speak anymore in His name.' But His word was in my heart like a burning fire shut up in my bones; I was weary of holding it back, And I could not." Jeremiah 20:8-9 NKJV

Yahweh was insistent that Jeremiah was not going to quit. This passage has nothing to do with deception. It deals with being persuaded.

Allah causes men to sin so that he can destroy them.

"And when we desire to destroy a city, *We command its men who live at ease, and they commit ungodliness therein*, then the word is realized against it, and we destroy it utterly." S. 17:16

Again let's make a normal, face value interpretation of this verse from the Qur'an. The obvious interpretation is that Allah commands men to sin in order to destroy them completely. The free will of the men in the city seems to be nonexistent. It seems that they are not even given the opportunity to repent and turn to Allah. This shows an absolute unconcern for the souls of these men. This is a stark contrast to the Yahweh's attitude of grace toward Sodom, Gomorrah, and Nineveh. Yahweh offered an opportunity to repent.

To make matters worse, he even ordains the evil that one commits. A Muslim saying *(Hadith)* points to this idea. This *Hadith* is from Abu Huraira. According to Abu Huraira, Mohammed said:

"Allah has written for the son of Adam his inevitable share of adultery whether he is aware of it or not: The adultery of the eye is the looking (at something which is sinful to look at), and the adultery of the tongue is to utter (what it is unlawful to utter), and the inner self wishes and longs for (adultery) and the private parts turn that into reality or refrain from submitting to the temptation." (*Ahadith*, collected by Sahih Al-Bukhari, Volume 8, Book 77, Number 609)

If we digest the information in this quote, it becomes apparent that Allah causes adultery. This is exactly the opposite of the Bible. The God of the Bible does not say that He causes adultery and that it is inevitable. He says:

"You shall not commit adultery." Exodus 20:14

A Muslim may ask, "What about the places in the Bible that say Yahweh intended to do evil to certain nations and individuals?" The Muslim might be referring to 2 Samuel 17:14. That passage says,

"...that the Lord might bring evil upon Absalom." (KJV)

The "evil" Yahweh poured out upon Absalom and Jeremiah was not immorality like that of the Qur'an. Instead it was judgment upon them due to their persistence in sin and refusal to repent.

In contrast to alternate translations of Hebrew words, the Arabic word **makara** does not allow for other possible meanings. Along with this linguistic idea, the Qur'an itself gives examples of Allah actually using deception and causing men to sin in order to fulfill his will! These examples move well beyond a small issue concerning possible translations.

Allah can abrogate (amend, revise, or change) his word.

According to the Qur'an, Allah reveals a verse only to have it canceled out a short time later:

"None of Our revelations do We abrogate or cause to be forgotten but We substitute something better or similar– Knowest thou not that Allah has power over all things?" S. 2:106

"When We substitute one revelation for another–and Allah knowest best what He reveals (in stages)–They say, "Thou art but a forger"; But most of them understand not. S." 16:101

This leaves the reader in a tough spot. The difficulty is having a god who does not remain consistent and often changes his revealed purpose. An obvious question arises. How is one to know that the promises concerning eternal security can be trusted? Just as he changes his mind in relation to the revelation, he can also decide to change his mind in regard to the believer's ultimate destiny without anything stopping him from doing so.

This is different from the Yahweh of the Holy Bible. He does not change and can be totally trusted in fulfilling all His promises:

"God is not a man that he should lie, nor a son of man that he should repent. Has he said, and will he not do? Or has he spoken, and will he not make it good?" Numbers 23:19

"For I, Yahweh, do not change." Malachi 3:6

"If we are faithless, he remains faithful; he cannot deny himself." 2 Timothy 2:13

"Jesus Christ is the same yesterday, today, and forever." Hebrews 13:8

Because the God of the Bible is immutable he can promise:

"Heaven and earth will pass away but my words will never pass away." Matthew 24:35

Allah confuses history.

In S. 17:1 we are told that Mohammed was taken to the farthest Mosque, *Masjid al-Aqsa*. This mosque is located in Jerusalem. The problem is that this mosque was not built until AD 691. That is after Mohammed's death in AD 632.

Unlike the Qur'an, the Bible seems to be purposefully set in history. The Bible almost asks for historians and archeologists to verify its historical contexts. Unlike the Qur'an, the Bible contains no proven historical errors. As of yet, archeology has failed to furnish credible evidence against any event recorded in the Bible. Some attacks center on the precise dating of archeological findings which a few see as contradicting the Bible's chronology. However, one cannot say that the Holy Bible is in error when archeologists themselves are divided over the precise dating of certain discoveries. There are many archeologists who provide evidence which they feel proves that the data fits perfectly with the Bible's dating of the events in question. We can be confident that archeology consistently verifies the Bible's accuracy.

Not one archeological discovery has ever proven the Bible wrong. Discovery after discovery has demonstrated the amazing historical accuracy of Scripture. The following quotations from a couple of the world's leading archeologists affirm this:

> "Nowhere has archeological discovery refuted the Bible as history." [2]

> "Near Eastern archeology has demonstrated the historical and geographical reliability of the Bible in many important areas. By clarifying the objectivity and factual accuracy of biblical authors, archeology also helps correct the view that the Bible is avowedly partisan and subjective. It is now known, for instance, that, along with the Hittites, Hebrew scribes were the best historians in the entire ancient Near East, despite contrary propaganda that emerged from Assyria, Egypt, and elsewhere." [3]

The late William F. Albright, one of the world's foremost archeologists, stated:

> "There can be no doubt that archeology has confirmed the substantial historicity of Old Testament tradition." [4]

Historical inaccuracy points to the idea that Allah is not omniscient. If he were omniscient, he could perfectly recall history.

Allah promises sexual pleasures to devoted followers.

The Qur'anic Paradise is totally different from the biblical portrait of heaven. In Allah's Paradise, there are sexual pleasures for believers to enjoy for eternity:

"But give glad tidings to those who believe and work righteousness, that their portions is Gardens, beneath which rivers flow, every time they are fed with fruits there from, they say: "Why, this is what we were fed with before," for they are giving things in similitude; And they have therein damsels (Arabic – *Houris* from which we get the English word "whore") pure (and holy); and they abide therein (forever)." S. 2:25

"But to those who believe and do deeds of righteousness, We shall soon admit to Gardens, with rivers flowing beneath, their eternal home. Therein they have damsels pure and holy; We shall admit them to shades, cool and ever deepening." S. 4:57

"Of a rare creation have We created the Houris, and We have made them *ever virgins,* dear to their spouses, of equal age with them for the people of the right hand." S. 56:35-38

"But for those who fear Allah is a blissful abode, enclosed gardens and vineyards, *and damsels with swelling breasts (Arabic – Kawa'eb),* their peers in age, and a full cup." S. 78:31-34

The standard orthodox Islamic understanding of these references is that Muslim men will have a host of large breasted maidens as sex-partners who return to their virginal state after intercourse. Obviously the focus is on male pleasure.

The eternal life of the Bible does not focus on such sensual pleasure. Human bodies are not the focus. The infinite love and joy of God is the focus. Hence, the believers' reward is to dwell with God forever in eternal glory:

"Jesus answered and said to them, 'The sons of this age marry and are given in marriage. But those who are counted worthy to attain that age and the resurrection from the dead, *neither marry nor are given in marriage*; nor can they die anymore for they are equal to the angels and are sons of God, being sons of the resurrection." Luke 20:34-36

"The kingdom of God is not food or drink, but righteousness, peace and joy in the Holy Spirit." Romans 14:17

"And I heard a loud voice from heaven saying, 'Behold, the tabernacle of God is with men, and He will dwell with them, and they shall be His people. God Himself will be with them and be their God. And God will wipe away every tear from their eyes; *there shall be no more death, nor sorrow, nor crying. There shall be no more pain,* for the former things have passed away." Revelation 21:3-4

Allah swears oaths by things lesser than himself.

To swear is to call upon something greater than yourself. A person swears an oath by invoking the name of something greater than himself. The implication is that the "something greater" will somehow force you to keep your promise or tell the truth. Allah swears by practically anything and everything, while Yahweh swears only by Himself. This makes it very difficult for the two to be the one and the same God. This is a real point of difference between Allah and Yahweh. Yahweh swears by *Himself*, since there is nothing greater for Him to swear by:

"For when God made a promise to Abraham, because *He could swear by no one greater,* He swore by Himself." Hebrews 6:13

"For men indeed swear by the greater, and an oath for confirmation is for them an end of all dispute." Hebrews 6:16

Every time God makes a pledge He swears only by Himself to insure believers that He will do all that He promises:

"I have sworn by Myself; the word has gone out of My mouth in righteousness, and shall not return, that to Me every knee shall bow. . ." Isaiah 45:23

"I swear by Myself, says the LORD." Jeremiah 22:5

In contrast to Yahweh, Allah swears by things other than himself. By the definition of an oath, this implies that Allah views those things as greater than himself.

- Allah swears by the Qur'an

  "By the Qur'an, full of wisdom." S. 36:2
  "By the Qur'an, full of admonition." S. 38:1

- Allah swears by the sky and constellations.

  "By the sky and the night visitant" S. 86:1
  "Nay verily: By the moon, and by the night as it retreateth, and by the dawn as it shines forth." S. 74:32-34
  "By the star when it goes down." S. 53:1

- Allah swears by the pen.

  "By the pen and by the record which [men] write." S. 68:1

- Allah swears by the Creation.

  "By the night as it cancels [the light]; by the day as it appears in glory; by the Creation of male and female." S. 92:1-3

Allah is not Triune.

The final proof that Allah is not Yahweh of the Bible is that Allah is not a trinity. According to the Holy Bible, there is only one true God:

"Hear O Israel! The LORD is our God. The LORD is one. And you shall love the LORD your God with all your heart and with all your soul and with all your might." Deuteronomy 6:4
"God is *only* One." Galatians 3:20.

At the same time Scripture affirms that there is only one God, Scripture also shows us that the One God eternally exists in three Persons. These persons are Father, Son, and Holy Spirit. All three are mentioned by Christ Himself in Matthew 28:19-20:

> "Go therefore and make disciples of all the nations, baptizing them in the name of the Father and the Son and the Holy Spirit, teaching them to observe all that I commanded you..."

All three members of the Trinity are present in Matthew 3:16-17:

> "And after being baptized, Jesus went up immediately from the water; and behold, the heavens were opened, and he saw the Spirit of God descending as a dove, and coming upon Him, and behold, a voice out of the heavens, saying, 'This is My beloved Son, in whom I am well pleased.'"

The Christian concept of the Trinity also makes the Christian God a God of relationship. In contrast, Allah is not a god who values relationship like the triune God of the Bible. He is not any of the three persons mentioned above. Surah 112 states:

> "Say: He is Allah, the One and Only; Allah, The Eternal, Absolute, *He begetteth not, nor is He Begotten*; and there is none like unto Him."

That Allah does not "beget" means that Allah has no children either in a spiritual or carnal sense. Thus, Allah can never be the Father. Nor does he allow himself to be "begotten", i.e. does not take on human nature such as God the Son did when He became man. Finally, in orthodox Islam, the Holy Spirit is the angel Gabriel, not God. This fact separates Allah from ever possibly being the same God that Christians worship.

Muslims deny the concept of a Trinity. A key passage here is I John 2:22-23:

"Who is the liar but the one who denies that Jesus is the Christ? *This is the Antichrist, the one who denies the Father and the Son.* Whoever denies the Son does not have the Father either; the one who confesses the Son has the Father also."

From these verses we see that Christians cannot believe that Allah is the biblical God if Allah is not a triune being.

Summary of Father Allah

- Allah schemes and deceives men.
- Allah sets men up to sin so he can destroy them.
- Allah selfishly changes his mind without concern for how it affects others.
- Allah focuses on sexual pleasures for his followers.
- Allah's oaths imply his inferiority.
- Allah does not value relationship.

This makes him a bad dad!

What Kind of Dad is "Heavenly Father Elohim?"

The Church of Jesus Christ of Latter-day Saints refers to a Heavenly Father named Elohim. Elohim is a biblical name for God the Father. They use the name but they have some peculiar beliefs about their Elohim that they do not talk about freely. The LDS church does not teach newcomers the peculiar doctrines. Recently I had breakfast with two young Mormon missionaries. We talked about the teaching that their god was once a man who became god. One of the missionaries agreed that they do believe this, but they do not share "deeper truth" with people who are first embracing Mormonism. The missionaries reserve that deep truth for later "when the convert is ready for it." Their method is to wait until a convert has learned to "trust the church and the living prophet" before they are told what the early LDS prophets taught as truth. It is as though there is a secret about Dad that must stay secret for as long as possible. This is the LDS missionary *modus operandi (MO)*.

This bears out in my personal experience with Mormons. Not all of them are instructed in their beliefs. Regular Mormon folk may not deny their doctrines, but they are often unaware of them. Let me give you one illustration. When I lived in Utah I was active in the local Civil Air Patrol as a search and rescue pilot. It was great mountain flying! I developed many friendships through this community involvement. One friendship was with a fellow pilot who wanted me to convert to Mormonism. We talked for hours as we flew to and from search grids. No, we did not talk religion while we were doing grid searches. We searched!

As I think back on all those conversations, I realize that I spent much time telling him what he should have known as a good Mormon. I would say things like, "You believe that God was a man who lived on another planet somewhere and achieved godhood." He would say, "No way, we don't believe that." Then I would instruct him in Mormon beliefs and follow up with what the Bible teaches. This Mormon was uninformed about Mormon doctrines.

It is valuable to know what they believe. A point I could make with my pilot friend is that one of us was uninformed. He was not only uninformed about the message I was sharing with him, he was uninformed about what his own church teaches. I hope our discussions gave me and my message a bit more credibility. Please note that the real point of a conversation about religion is NOT to win the argument. It is to win the person!

The Mormon Arrow Points UP

A good illustration of the Mormon concept of God is an arrow that points up. Their god, the god who created the Universe as we know it, has not always been god. They think he started as a man and achieved "godhood." This is an arrow pointing up toward "godhood." On the other hand, the Bible teaches that God became a man. The Bible arrow points down.

As we look at their beliefs, you will notice constant references to their source documents. Like my pilot friend, not every Mormon knows what their church believes. I reference the documents so that you can see where the beliefs are taught.

Mormon Theology Proper

1. God started as a man.

According to Mormon documents and accepted sources, God (*Elohim*) used to be a man on another planet.

- "God himself was once as we are now, and is an exalted man, and sits enthroned in yonder heavens!!! . . . We have imagined that God was God from all eternity. I will refute that idea and take away the veil, so that you may see" (*Teachings of the Prophet Joseph Smith*, p. 345)
- God the Father had a Father, (Joseph Smith, *History of the Church*, vol. 6, p. 476; Heber C. Kimball, Journal of Discourses, vol. 5, p. 19; Milton Hunter, First Council of the Seventy, *The Gospel Through the Ages*, p. 104-105.)
- God resides near a star called Kolob, (*Pearl of Great Price*, pages 34-35; Mormon Doctrine, p. 428.)
- God had sexual relations with Mary to make the body of Jesus, (Brigham Young, *Journal of Discourses*, Vol. 4, p. 218, 1857; vol. 8, p. 115.). This one is disputed among many Mormons and not always 'officially' taught or believed. Nevertheless, Young, the 2nd prophet of the Mormon Church taught it.
- "Therefore we know that both the Father and the Son are in form and stature perfect men; each of them possesses a tangible body . . . of flesh and bones." (*Articles of Faith*, by James Talmage, p. 38).
- "The Father has a body of flesh and bones as tangible as man's. . ." (*D&C* 130:22).
- God is in the form of a man, (Joseph Smith, *Journal of Discourses*, Vol. 6, p. 3.)

2. This man became god.

Christians say that Jesus is the God-man. Mormons could flip that and say that their god is a Man-God. Mormons believe that through obedience and devotion to the Mormon faith every man has the potential to become a god, (*Teachings of the Prophet Joseph Smith,* pages 345-347, 354.)

"Then shall they be gods, because they have no end; therefore shall they be from everlasting to everlasting, because they continue; then shall they be above all, because all things are subject unto them. Then shall they be gods, because they have all power, and the angels are subject unto them," (D&C 132:20).

Joseph Smith taught this doctrine in April of 1844:

"God himself was once as we are now, and is an exalted man, and sits enthroned in yonder heavens! That is the great secret. If the veil were rent today, and the great God who holds this world in its orbit, and who upholds all worlds and all things by His power, was to make himself visible, — I say, if you were to see him today, you would see him like a man in form–like yourselves in all the person, image, and very form as a man. . . .

. . . It is the first principle of the gospel to know for a certainty the character of God, and to know that we may converse with Him as one man converses with another, and that He was once a man like us; yea, that God himself, the Father of us all, dwelt on an earth, the same as Jesus Christ Himself did." (Smith, *History of the Church,* 6:305)

The fifth LDS president was Lorenzo Snow. He was president from 1898 to 1901. He coined a summary statement of Mormon theology that says:

"As man now is, God once was; As God now is, man may be." *(The Teachings of Lorenzo Snow*, comp. Clyde J. Williams, Salt Lake City: Bookcraft, 1984)

In a recent conversation with Mormon missionaries, one of the young men said that this is how it is taught today. Now, they say:

"As you (man) are he (god) once was; As he (god) is you (man) can be."

Mormons believe that when god was a man on a planet some-where around an imaginary star called Kolob, he was a good Mormon. He attained perfection through long periods of growth, development, and progression "by going from one small degree to another, and from a small capacity to a great one; from grace to grace, from exaltation to exaltation." Joseph Smith used the illustra-tion of a ladder to teach this. He said:

"When you climb up a ladder, you must begin at the bottom, and ascend step by step, until you arrive at the top; and so it is with the principles of the gospel–you must begin with the first, and go on until you learn all the principles of exaltation. But it will be a great while after you have passed through the veil before you will have learned them. It is not all to be comprehended in this world; it will be a great work to learn our salvation and exaltation even beyond the grave." *(The Teachings of Lorenzo Snow*, comp. Clyde J. Williams: Salt Lake City: Bookcraft, 1984)

Remember, the Mormon arrow points up but the Bible arrow points down. The Bible teaches that God is the same from eternity to eternity.

". . .the Father of lights, *with Whom is no variableness, neither shadow of turning.*" James 1:17
"Jesus Christ the same yesterday, and today, and forever." Hebrews 13:8

How do Mormon folk square what the Bible says about God being "from everlasting to everlasting" with the idea that he has not always been God? First, they believe that biblical passages that speak of God's eternality and of his being the same yesterday, today, and forever make reference ONLY to His divine attributes such as his love, constancy, and willingness to bless his people.

Mormons believe that god was once a man and that over a long period of time he gained the knowledge, power, and divine attributes necessary to know all things and have all power. Because he has held his exalted status for a longer period than any of us can conceive, he is able to speak in terms of eternity and can state that he is from everlasting to everlasting. President Joseph Fielding Smith said,

"From eternity to eternity means from the spirit existence through the probation which we are in, and then back again to the eternal existence which will follow. Surely this is everlasting, for when we receive the resurrection, we will never die. We all existed in the first eternity. I think I can say of myself and others, we are from eternity; and we will be to eternity everlasting, if we receive the exaltation." (Joseph Fielding Smith, *Doctrines of Salvation*, comp. Bruce R. McConkie, 3 vols. Salt Lake City: Bookcraft, 1954-56, 1:12; and see Bruce R. McConkie, *The Promised Messiah*, Salt Lake City: Deseret Book, 1978, 166)

Mormons think that seeing god as an exalted man makes them more confident when they pray. This is a misinterpretation of Hebrews 4:15:

"For we do not have a high priest who cannot sympathize with our weaknesses, but One who has been tempted in all things as we are, yet without sin."

Joseph seems to have missed the "without sin" part of the verse. The man in his "man who became god" theology would have been guilty of sins. Joseph's successor, Brigham Young, taught that the Father in Heaven

"has passed the ordeals we are now passing through; he has received an experience, has suffered and enjoyed, and knows all that we know regarding the toils, sufferings, life and death of this mortality, for he has passed through the whole of it, and has received his crown and exaltation." (*Journal of Discourses*, 26 vols. (Liverpool: F. D. Richards & Sons, 1851-86), 11:249; see 7:333)

Mormons say that this means they can pray to him with the perfect assurance that he understands their struggles completely. Because he was a man he can empathize with us. His experience as a man adds to his omniscient and all-loving capacity to righteously judge his children. He has a body and passions. They say that this makes him approachable and knowable. The trouble is that it also makes him guilty of sin because he would have been unholy when he was a man.

Mormons believe that the ancients had this knowledge of god's origin but lost it. They say it has been restored through modern prophets. Mormons teach that men and women may come to understand their own eternal identities and divine possibilities just as god did.

3. This Man-god has a Woman-god Wife

Mormons also believe that the man who became god has a wife. This wife is a heavenly mother-goddess too. She is described first as mother because she and god have children.

"God is married to his goddess wife and has spirit children..." (*Mormon Doctrine*, p. 516.)

This is not Biblical! Remember, Mormons believe that their leaders are continuously receiving new truth from God. To them, that new truth is just as authoritative as the Bible. The Heavenly Mother idea is not found in the Bible. It is one of the "new truths."

Latter-day Saints believe that all the people of earth who lived or will live are actually spirit babies resulting from this union. Since parenthood requires both father and mother, they believe that the "father and mother" are constantly busy making spiritual babies who live in what Mormons call the "pre-mortal life." They believe that these spirit babies are in need of "physical tabernacles" (bodies) on earth. This is one reason why Mormon families are so large.

The Heavenly Mother also must have been a good woman. Mormons are logical in that if the Heavenly Father was a man who achieved godhood through obedience and devotion, then the Heavenly Mother ALSO must have been a woman who somehow achieved godhood through obedience and devotion. If her status is not officially godhood she is at least exalted to the high position of eternally pregnant sex partner. LDS believe that she is like their "heavenly father" in glory, perfection, compassion, wisdom, and holiness.

Does that sound similar to another religious belief? Doesn't that sound like the Roman Catholic view of Mary? We can look at this in two ways. First, we can see this Mormon heavenly mother idea as a fingerprint of Satan that shows up in many other cults and religions not based on Bible truth. Or, we can give Joseph Smith "credit" for it. Remember, Joseph had a way of borrowing ideas from existing religious thought as he developed his own doctrine.

Practically speaking, the Mormon concept of eternal family is more than a take-it-or-leave-it belief. It influences their way of life. It is part of their eternal plan of life that stretches from life *before* through life *beyond* mortality. Family is crucial in their theology. They believe that their earthly family (husbands, wives, and children) will continue and expand in the afterlife. In fact a "Families Are Forever" bumper-sticker probably means that the driver is a Mormon. For more information you may refer to the *Encyclopedia of Mormonism, Vol. 2, Mother in Heaven.*

Let's leave the Mormon Mom and get back to the Bad Dad.

Mormon Speak explains Heavenly Father

This is how Mormon leaders teach that their god was once a man who achieved godhood.

1. Joseph Smith taught that God was once a mortal man.

> "*God himself was once as we are now, and is an exalted man*, and sits enthroned in yonder heavens! That is *the great secret... I am going to tell you how God came to be God. We have imagined and supposed that God was God from all eternity. I will refute that idea*, and take away the veil...
>
> "It is the first principle of the gospel to know for a certainty the character of God. . .and that *He was once a man like us; yea, that God himself, the Father of us all, dwelt on an earth, the same as Jesus Christ Himself did . . .you have got to learn how to be gods yourselves*, and to be kings and priests to God, the same as all gods have done before you, namely, by going from one small degree to another. . . *from exaltation to exaltation*, until you attain to the resurrection of the dead, and are able to dwell in everlasting burnings and to sit in glory, as do those who sit enthroned in everlasting power." (*History of the Church*, Vol.6, Ch.14, p.305-6)

2. Brigham Young taught that God was once a finite being.

> "It appears ridiculous to the world, under their darkened and erroneous traditions, that *God has once been a finite being*" (*Deseret News*, Nov.16, 1859, p.290).

3. Joseph Fielding Smith said that God had a father, a grandfather, etc..

> "Our *father in heaven*, according to the Prophet, *had a father*, and since there has been a condition of this kind through all eternity, *each Father had a Father*" (*Doctrines of Salvation*, 2:47).

"I know that God is a being with body, parts and passions. . .Man was born of woman; Christ, the Savior, was born of woman; and *God, the Father was born of woman*" (*Deseret News*, Church News, Sept.19, 1936, p.2).

4. LDS Apostle Bruce R. McConkie continues this teaching.

"The Father is a glorified, perfected, *resurrected, exalted man who worked out his salvation by obedience* to the same laws he has given to us so that we may do the same" (*A New Witness for the Articles of Faith*, p.64)

5. LDS Apostle Melvin Ballard explained that God has a wife.

"For as we have *a Father in heaven*, so also we have a *Mother* there, a glorified, exalted, ennobled *Mother*" (As quoted in *Achieving a Celestial Marriage*, LDS Church manual, 1976, p.129).

6. LDS leaders teach that faithful Mormons can achieve godhood.

"Intelligent beings are organized *to become Gods*, even the Sons of God, to dwell in the *presence of the Gods*, and become associated with the highest intelligences that dwell in eternity. We are now in the school, and must practice upon what we receive" (*Discourses of Brigham Young*, p.245).

"We are *precisely* in the *same condition* and under the *same circumstances that God* our heavenly Father was *when he was passing through this, or a similar ordeal*" (*Gospel Doctrine*, p.54).

"We believe in a God who is Himself *progressive*, whose majesty is intelligence; whose perfection consists *in eternal advancement*–a Being who has *attained* His exalted state by a path which now His children are permitted to follow, whose glory it is their heritage to share. *In spite of the opposition of the sects, in the face of direct charges of blasphemy, the Church proclaims the eternal truth: 'As man is, God once was; as God is, man may be'*" (*Articles of Faith*, Ch.24, p.430 – p.431).

7. *Doctrine and Covenants* promises that devoted LDS couples can become gods too.

"…if a *man marry a wife*, and make a covenant with her *for time and for all eternity*… they shall [have] …a *continuation of the seeds* [children] forever and ever. Then shall they *be gods*, because they have no end; therefore shall they be from everlasting to everlasting… Then shall they *be gods*, because they have all power… and *continuation of the lives*… [endless procreation of spirit children]" D & C 132:18-22.

"Father Elohim" from the Quad

- If God is as the Mormons claim, then he was guilty of some unrighteousness first, because he was once a man!
- If God is as the Mormons claim, then he is guilty of incest. He had a physical, sexual relationship with Mary (his own spirit child).
- If God is as the Mormons claim, then he is guilty of adultery against his Heavenly Wife because he had sex with Mary to produce Jesus' body.

This makes him a bad dad!

What Kind of Dad is "Abba?"

Born-Again believers may refer to God the Father using *"abba"* as a term that denotes a sense of closeness. The word is from Aramaic and can be understood best by thinking of what "daddy" means in English. *Abba* is not disrespectful. Rather, it denotes a tender warmth and dependence free of fear and anxiety. This is the term used in Scripture:

"For you have not received a spirit of slavery leading to fear again, but you have *received a spirit of adoption as sons by which we cry out, 'Abba! Father!'* The Spirit Himself bearing witness with our spirit that we are the children of God" Romans 8:15

1. GOD has always been God. He was not a man who became god.

"Art thou not from everlasting, O Lord my God, mine Holy One?" Hab. 1:12

"For I am the Lord, I change not." Mal. 3:6

". . .from everlasting to everlasting, thou art God." Psa. 90:2

"God is not a man, that he should lie; neither the son of man, that he should repent." Num. 23:19

"Professing themselves to be wise, they became fools, and changed the glory of the incorruptible God into an image made like to corruptible man,. . .who changed the truth of God into a lie, and worshipped and served the creature more than the Creator, who is blessed for ever." Rom. 1:22-25

- *The LDS god started as a finite man and progressed to godhood.*
- *Bible: GOD has always been God.*

2. GOD has always been holy. He was not a sinful man in the past.

". . .a God of truth and without iniquity, just and right is he." Deut. 32:4

"I am God, and not man; the Holy One in the midst of thee." Hos. 11:9

"The Lord is righteous in all his ways and holy in all his works." Psa. 145:17

"God is light, and in him is no darkness at all." 1 John 1:5

"Thy righteousness is an everlasting righteousness." Psa. 119:142

- *The LDS god achieved holiness.*
- *GOD has always been holy.*

3. GOD has always been omniscient (all knowing).

"Who hath directed the Spirit of the Lord, or being his counselor hath taught him? With whom took he counsel, and who instructed him, and taught him knowledge, and shewed to him the way of understanding? . . . There is no searching of his understanding." Isa. 40:13,14,28

"Great is our Lord, and of great power: his understanding is infinite." Psa. 147:5

- *The LDS god had to learn everything.*
- *GOD has always been omniscient.*

4. GOD has always been omnipotent (all powerful).

"The Lord God omnipotent reigneth." Rev. 19:6

". . .His eternal power and Godhead." Rom. 1:20

- *The LDS god attained his power*
- *GOD has always been omnipotent.*

5. GOD is Omnipresent.

"The heaven is my throne, and the earth is my footstool; where is the house that ye build unto me: and where is the place of my .rest?" Isa. 66:1

"Am I a God at hand, saith the Lord, and not a God afar off? Can any hide himself in secret places that I shall not see him? Saith the Lord. Do not I fill heaven and earth? Saith the Lord." Jer. 23:23-24

- *The LDS god can be in only one place at a time*
- *GOD is omnipresent.*

6. GOD is Self-sufficient (not dependent on anything).

"I am the Lord that maketh all things; that stretcheth forth the heavens alone, that spreadeth abroad the earth by myself." Isa. 44:24

"By the word of the Lord were the heavens made; and all the host of them by the breath of his mouth." Psa. 33:6

"Thou hast made heaven, the heaven of heavens, with all their host, the earth, and all things that are therein, the seas, and all that is therein, and thou preservest them all." Neh. 9:6

- *The LDS god cooperated with the "Council of Gods" to create.*
- *GOD is Self-sufficient (not dependent on anything).*

7. GOD is unique and unequaled.

"I am he; before me there was no God formed neither shall there be after me. I, even I, am the Lord; and beside me there is no savior." Isa. 43:10-11

"I am the first, and I am the last; and beside me there is no God. . ..is there a God beside me; yea, there is no God; I know not any." Isa. 44:6&8

"To whom will ye liken me, and make me equal, and compare me, that we may be like?. . .for I am God, and there is none else; I am God, and there is none like me." Isa. 46:5,9

"I am the Lord; that is my name; and my glory will I not give to another." Isa. 42:8

- *The LDS god has a father, grandfather, brothers and sisters, etc.*
- *GOD is unique and unequaled.*

Chapter Conclusion

The fingerprints we examined identify the LDS Heavenly Father and the Muslim Allah. In some ways Mormons and Muslims worship the same kind of Father. But, the prints point away from the Father of the Bible. The Christian God is not the Mormon Heavenly Father. The Christian God is not Allah. Christians, Mormons and Muslims do not worship the same God.

Chapter 4

Questions for Discussion

1 How does one's earthly father influence feelings about our Heavenly Father?
2 What would you think of an earthly dad who was like Allah? Mormon Elohim?
3 Is it possible to get too familiar and comfortable with Abba Father?

Chapter 5

Checking Their Christs' Matching Fingerprints

Is Jesus Satan's Brother? Is Jesus Just Another Prophet?

In Matthew 16:12-14, Jesus asked the disciples a question. He asked, "Who do men say that I am?" Later He asked the same question in a more pointed and personal way. He asked, "Who do YOU say that I am?" His point was to get them to think about who He was.

In this section we will use that question as a launching point to see what Muslims and Mormons believe about Jesus Christ. We will ask, "Who do Muslim men say that I am?" Then we'll ask, "Who do Mormon men say that I am?" We also will include a brief look at what the Bible says.

This section includes many quotations. Rather than repeat "emphasis mine" after every quotation, please note that *italicized text* in quotations and citations indicates the emphasis placed by the author.

Who do Muslims say that I (Jesus) am?

Here are fifteen statements that describe how Muslim men view Jesus. Each is followed by a biblical response. Although volumes could be written about each of the statements, the point here is for us to see that these ideas about Jesus come from their source documents. These two sources, the *Qur'an* and *Hadiths,* are the ultimate authority in the Muslim religion.

1. Muslim men say that Jesus was created and not eternal.

- "The similitude of Jesus before Allah is that of Adam: he created him from dust, and then said to him, 'Be': and he was." Sura 3:59

The Bible teaches that Jesus is eternal and uncreated.

- "In the beginning was the Word and the Word was with God, and the Word was God. . .the Word (Jesus) became flesh and dwelt among us ." John. 1:1, 14

2. Muslim men say that Jesus was not crucified.

- "That they said (in boast), 'we killed Christ Jesus the son of Mary, the Messenger of Allah.' But they killed him not, nor crucified him, but so it was made to appear to them, and those who differ therein are full of doubts, with no (certain) knowledge, but only conjecture to follow, for of surety they killed him not. . .." Surah 4:157

The Bible record is clear that Jesus died on a cross, was buried, and rose again. (John 20)

3. Muslim men say that Jesus experienced Assumption not Resurrection.

- "And because of their saying (in boast), 'We killed Messiah 'Eesa (Jesus), son of Maryam (Mary), the Messenger of Allah,' but they killed him not, nor crucified him, but it appeared so to them the resemblance of 'Eesa (Jesus) was put over another man (and they killed that man), and those who differ therein are full of doubts. They have no (certain) knowledge, they follow nothing but conjecture. For surely; they killed him not [i.e. 'Eesa (Jesus), son of Maryam (Mary)]: *But Allah raised him ['Eesa (Jesus]) up (with his body and soul) unto Himself (and he is in the heavens).* And Allah is Ever All Powerful, All Wise." S 4:157-158

The Bible teaches that Jesus was crucified and resurrected.

- "I make known to you the Gospel. . .Christ died for our sins according to the Scriptures, and that He was buried, and that He was raised on the third day according to the Scriptures." I Corinthians 15:1, 3-4

4. Muslim men say that Jesus prophesied the coming of Mohammed.

- "And (remember) when 'Eesa (Jesus), son of Maryam (Mary), said: 'O Children of Israel! I am the Messenger of Allah unto you, confirming the Tawraat [(Torah) which came] before me, and giving glad tidings of a Messenger to *come* after me, whose name shall be Ahmad.' But when he (Ahmad, i.e. Mohammed) came to them with clear proofs, they said: 'This is plain magic'." Sura 61:6

The Bible never mentions Mohammed. Mohammed is suggesting this memory.

5. Muslim men say that salvation is found in their Five Pillars, NOT in Jesus.

- They teach that salvation can be found only in the Five Pillars of Shahada (Testifying of God's Oneness), Salat (Prayer), Saum (Fasting), Zakat (Charity), and Hajj (Pilgrimage). This is an Islamic basic.
- "Those who believe, and suffer exile and strive (*jahadu*) with might and main in Allah's cause, with their goods and their

persons, have the highest rank in the sight of Allah. They are the people who will achieve salvation. Those who believe, and emigrate and strive with might and main, in Allah's cause, with their goods and their persons, have the highest rank in the sight of Allah: they are the people who will achieve (salvation)." S 9:20-22

- "If any do deeds of righteousness, be they male or female, and have faith, they will enter Heaven, and not the least injustice will be done to them." Surah 4:124

The Bible teaches that Jesus is the only way.

- "He is the stone which was rejected by you, the builders, but which became the very corner stone. And *there is salvation in no one else*; for *there is no other name under heaven* that has been given among men, by which we must be saved." Acts 4:11-12
- "For by grace you have been saved through *faith*; and that *not of yourselves,* it is the gift of God; *not as a result of works* that no one should boast." Ephesians 2:8,9
- "The *blood* of Jesus Christ his Son *cleanses us from all sin"* 1 John 1:7.
- *He saved us not on the basis of deeds which we have done in righteousness,* but according to his mercy." Titus 3:5

    6. **Muslim men say that Jesus was an involuntary Slave to Allah.**

- "Jesus, although he is just one of Allah's slaves..."
- "I will then say what the Pious Slave Jesus the son of Mary said. . .(Hadith: Narrated by Ibn Abbas 5.117-118).
- "You'd better go to Jesus, Allah's slave." (Hadith: Narrated by Anas, Volume 9, Book 93, Number 507.)

The Bible teaches that Jesus is King of Kings and Lord of Lords.

- "And on His robe and on His thigh He has a name written, 'King of kings, and Lord of lords.' " Revelation 19:16

7. Muslim men say that Jesus is not God in the flesh.

- "Surely, they have disbelieved who say: Allah is the Messiah ['Eesa (Jesus)], son of Maryam (Mary)'" Surah 5:72
- "Surely, disbelievers are those who said: 'Allah is the third of the three (in a Trinity)." But there is no Allah (god) (none who has the right to be worshipped) but One Allah (God—Allah). And if they cease not from what they say, verily, a painful torment will befall on the disbelievers among them." Surah 5:73
- "Then the sects differed i.e. the Christians about 'Eesa (Jesus), so woe unto the disbelievers those who gave false witness by saying that 'Eesa (Jesus) is the son of Allah from the Meeting of a great Day (i.e. the Day of Resurrection, when they will be thrown in the blazing Fire)." Surah 19:34-38
- "That they ascribe a son (or offspring or children) to the Most Gracious (Allah). But it is not suitable for (the Majesty of) the Most Gracious (Allah) that He should beget a son (or offspring or children). There is none in the heavens and the earth but comes unto the Most Gracious (Allah) as a slave." Surah 19:88-93
- "Glory be to Him: (far exalted is He) above having a son." Surah 4:171

The Bible teaches that Jesus was the eternal God who "became flesh."

- "For in Him all things were created, both in the heavens and the earth, visible and invisible, whether thrones or dominions or rulers or authorities—all things have been created through Him and for Him." Colossians 1:16

- "In the beginning was the Word and the Word was with God, and the Word was God. . .the Word (Jesus) became flesh and dwelt among us." John. 1:1, 14

8. Muslim men say that Jesus cannot be worshipped.

- "And behold, Allah will say—O Jesus Son of Mary, did you say to men, worship me and my mother as gods beside Allah? He will reply—Glory to you, I could never say what I had not the right [to say]. . ." Surah 5:116
- "Christ the son of Mary was no more than a messenger: many were the messengers that passed away before him." Surah 5:75

The Bible teaches that Jesus accepts worship because He is God.

- ". . .I heard the voice of many angels around the throne and the living creatures and the elders. . .saying with a loud voice. . .'Worthy is the Lamb that was slain to receive power and riches and wisdom and might and honor and glory and blessing.'" Revelation 5:12
- "And he (the healed man) said, 'Lord I believe.' And he worshiped Him (Jesus)" John 9:38

9. Muslim men say that Jesus, as mediator, is inferior to Mohammed.
- "They will go to Jesus who will say, 'I am not fit for this undertaking, but you'd better go to Mohammed whose sins of the past and future had been forgiven (by Allah).'" Hadith Volume 9, Book 93, Number 507.

The Bible teaches that Jesus is the one "mediator" with God the Father.

- "For there is one God and *one mediator* also between God and men: the Man Christ Jesus." 1 Tim. 2:5

10. Muslim men say that Jesus is just another prophet.

- "Jesus, and that given to (all) prophets from their Lord: We make no difference between one and another of them. . ." Surah 2.136, 2.84

The Bible teaches that Jesus is the Son of God, not just a prophet.

- "For God so loved the world, that He gave His only begotten Son, that whoever believes in Him should not perish, but have eternal life. For God did not send the Son into the world to judge the world, but that the world should be saved through Him." John 3:16-17

11. Muslim men say that Jesus will return wearing yellow garments.

- "Jesus (peace be upon him). He will descend (to the earth). When you see him, recognize him: a man of medium height, reddish fair, wearing two light yellow garments." (*Sunan*, Abu Dawud Book 37, Number 4310)

The Bible does not specify what color His garments will be.

12. Muslim men say that Jesus will return and touch the earth on a Minaret in Damascus.

- "Most Muslims believe that Jesus' descent from heaven will be accomplished by resting his hands on the wings of two angels. He will descend onto the white minaret, situated in the eastern part of Damascus. He will invite the whole world to be Muslim including Christians and Jews." (Mawdudi, A.A, *Finality of Prophethood*, pp. 58-61), and (Vol 18, Hadith No. 814)

The Bible teaches that Jesus will return to Jerusalem to touch the Mount of Olives.

- "And in that day His feet will stand on the Mount of Olives, which is in front of Jerusalem on the east. . ." Zechariah 14:4

13. Muslim men say that when Jesus returns He will kill the Jews.

- "When the Muslims will fall in lines to offer prayers, Christ, son of Mary, shall descend from heaven before their eyes. He will lead the prayers. When the prayers are over he will say to the people: "Clear the way between me and this enemy of God." God will give victory to the Muslims over the hosts of Dajjal (Antichrist). The Muslims will inflict dire punishment upon the enemy. Even the trees and stones will cry out, "O Abdullah, O Abdul Rahman, O Muslim, come, here is a Jew behind me, kill him." In this way *God will cause the Jews to be annihilated and Muslims shall be the victors.* " (recorded by Hafiz Ibn Hajar in *Fath-ul-Bari* Vol. VI, p. 450)

The Bible teaches that Jesus will judge the rebelling nations, not kill Jews.

- "And He is clothed with a robe dipped in blood; and His name is called The Word of God. . .and from His mouth comes a sharp sword, so that with it He may smite the nations (not Jews). . ." Revelation 5:13, 15
- Jews will "look upon Me (Jesus) who they pierced" as prophesied in Zechariah 12:10-14. They will turn to Jesus as their Messiah! Israel will not be annihilated.

14. Muslim men say that Jesus will marry and have children.

- "He (Jesus) will live for forty years during which he will marry, have children, and perform Hajj (pilgrimage). . ." (*Wali ad-*

Din, Miskat Al-Masabih, (tr. James Robson), Vol. II, p.1159; Sahih Muslim, Vol.1, p.92).

The Bible says nothing about Jesus being married.

15. Muslim men say that Jesus will die forty years after his return.

- "He (Jesus) will perish all religions except Islam. He (Jesus) will destroy the Antichrist and will live on the earth for forty years and then he will die. . ." "After his death, he will be buried beside the grave of the Prophet Mohammed (*Wali ad-Din*, Miskat Al-Masabih, (tr. James Robson), Vol. II, p.1159; *Sahih Muslim*, Vol.1, p.92).

The Bible teaches that Jesus died on the cross but is now raised and will live forever.

Clearly the Jesus of the Qur'an and the Hadiths is not the same Jesus of the Bible. There is a vast difference between these two persons. This should not be a surprise to Christians. Jesus warned that many would come and imitate Him. We should remember a warning that Jesus Christ Himself gave and repeated:

> "For false Christs and false prophets will arise and will show great signs and wonders so as to mislead, if possible, even the elect." Matthew 24:24
> "For false Christs and false prophets will arise and will show signs and wonders, in order, if possible, to lead the elect astray." Mark 13:22

Who do Mormons say that I (Jesus) am?

1. Mormon men say that Jesus was conceived by sexual intercourse.

They teach that there was a physical, bodily union between God the Father and Mary. Mormon Christology denies the Virgin Birth of Christ.

- Brigham Young taught: "The birth of the Savior was as *natural as are the births of our children*; it was the result of *natural action.* He partook of flesh and blood — was begotten of his Father as we were of our fathers," (*Religious Truths Defined,* Vol 8, p.115) and "when the Virgin Mary conceived the child Jesus, the Father had begotten him in his own likeness and blood. He was *not begotten by the Holy Ghost*" (*Religious Truths Defined,* vol.1, p.50).
- Brigham Young says: "I will say that I was naturally begotten; so was my father, and *also* my Savior Jesus Christ. . .he is the first begotten of his father in the flesh, and there was *nothing unnatural* about it" (*Religious Truths Defined,* vol.8, p.211); "Now remember from this time forth, and for ever, that *Jesus Christ was not begotten by the Holy Ghost*" (*Religious Truths Defined,*vol.1, p.51).
- LDS apostle Orson Pratt said: "the Father and *Mother of Jesus,* according to the flesh, must have been *associated together* in the capacity of Husband and Wife...as God was the first husband to her, it may be that He only gave her to be the wife of Joseph while in this mortal state, and that He intended after the resurrection to *again take her as one of his own wives* to raise up immortal spirits in eternity" (*Religious Truths Defined,* vol. 1, p.158, 1853).
- Joseph Fielding Smith, the fourth president of the LDS church, wrote: "The birth of the Savior was a *natural* occurrence *unattended by any degree of mysticism,* and the Father God was the *literal parent of Jesus in the flesh* as well as in the spirit"

This teaching is not just something Mormon folk believed during the early days of their church. More recent teachers still hold to the same positions about Jesus.

- Bruce McConkie (LDS apostle) states: "Christ was begotten by an Immortal Father *in the same way that mortal men are begotten* by mortal fathers" (*Mormon Doctrine*, p. 547, 1979).
- Carfred Broderick (Mormon author) writes: "God is a procreating personage of flesh and bone. . .Latter-day prophets have made it clear that despite what it says in Matthew 1:20, *the Holy Ghost was not the father of Jesus. . .The Savior was fathered by a personage of flesh and bone*" (Dialogue: A Journal of Mormon Thought, Autumn, 1967, p.100-101).

One might ask, "How can Mormon men still say that they believe in the Virgin Birth?" They can because they change the definition of the word "virgin." Mormons redefine many Christian words. They say that since Mary had sexual relations with an immortal man, not a mortal man, the phrase "virgin birth" still applies.

- McConkie explains: "Suffice it to say that our Lord was born of a **virgin**, which is fitting and proper, and *also natural,* since the Father of the Child was an **immortal** Being" (*The Promised Messiah*, p. 466).

In contrast, the Bible teaches that Jesus was miraculously conceived by the Holy Spirit, fulfilling Isaiah's prophecy that the Messiah would be born of a virgin:

- "The Lord Himself shall give you a sign: Behold a **virgin** will be with child and bear a son, and she will call His name Immanuel." Isaiah 7:14
- "Now the birth of Christ was as follows. When His mother Mary had been betrothed to Joseph, before they came together she was found to be with child *by the Holy Spirit*...for that

which was conceived in her is **of the Holy Spirit.**" Matthew 1:18,20

- "Mary said to the angel, 'How can this be, since I am a virgin?' And the angel answered and said to her, 'The *Holy Spirit will come upon you* and the power of the Most High will overshadow you.'" Luke 1:34-5

God intended that the birth of the Messiah would be a miraculous event. Like His resurrection, it would provide evidence to the skeptical and confirm that Jesus was indeed the Messiah.

2. Mormon men say that Lucifer is the brother of Jesus.

One attack on the uniqueness of Jesus is the Mormon teaching that Jesus and Lucifer are brothers. This teaching does two things. It lowers Jesus Christ's status as the unique Son of God. And it elevates Satan's importance to that of equality with Jesus.

- President Spencer W. Kimball wrote, "Long before you were born a program was developed by your creators . . . The principal personalities in this great drama were a Father Elohim, perfect in wisdom, judgment, and person, and *two sons, Lucifer and Jehovah*." (*Mormon Doctrine*, p. 32-33).
- James Talmage explains who Jehovah is: "*Jesus Christ was Jehovah. . .*Jesus Christ, who is the Jehovah of the Old Testament" (Doctrines of Salvation, vol.1, p.11, 27).
- Milton R. Hunter (an LDS General Authority) explains "The appointment of Jesus to be Savior of the world was contested by *one of the other sons of God. He was called Lucifer...this spirit-brother of Jesus* desperately tried to become the Savior of mankind" (*The Gospel Through the Ages*, p.15, 1945).
- Joseph Smith stated: "The contention in heaven was. . .Jesus said there would be certain souls that would not be saved; and the *Devil said he could save them all,* and laid his plans before the grand council, who gave their vote in favor of Jesus Christ. So the Devil rose up in rebellion against God, and was cast down" (*Journal of Discourses*, vol. 6, p. 8).

- "And Satan came among them, saying: *I am also a son of God*" (*Pearl of Great Price*, Moses 5:17).

In contrast the Bible describes Satan (Lucifer) as a created angelic being.

- "You (Lucifer) were in Eden, the garden of God…on the day that *you were created*…you were the anointed cherub…you were blameless in your ways from the day *you were created* until unrighteousness was found in you…your heart was lifted up…you corrupted your wisdom." Ezekiel 28:13,15,17

3. Mormon men say Jesus began as a spirit child.

They teach that Jesus was conceived first as a spirit child by the Heavenly Father and Heavenly Mother and was later conceived physically by the Heavenly Father and an earthly mother: (*The Ensign*, Jan. 1989, pp.28-29; *Come Unto Christ* by Ezra Taft Benson, p.4).

- Bruce McConkie states: "Christ the Word, the Firstborn, had of course attained unto the status of Godhood *while yet in pre-existence*" (*What Mormons Think of Christ*, p. 36).
- Bruce McConkie continues: "He is the Firstborn of the Father. By obedience and devotion to the truth he attained that pinnacle of intelligence which ranked him as a God, as the Lord Omnipotent, *while yet in his pre-existent state*" (*Mormon Doctrine*, 1966, p. 129).
- Orson Pratt: "God the Father had a plurality of wives, one or more being in eternity, by whom *He begat our spirits as well as the spirit of Jesus His First Born*" (*The Seer*, p. 172).
- "Jesus Christ is not the Father of the *spirits* who have taken or yet shall take bodies upon this earth, for *He is one of them*. He is The Son, as they are sons and daughters of Elohim." (*Encyclopedia of Mormonism*, vol.4, Appendix 4).

However, the Bible declares that Jesus has always existed and that all things were created through Him:

- "For in Him all things were created, both in the heavens and the earth, visible and invisible, whether thrones or dominions or rulers or authorities—all things have been created through Him and for Him." Colossians 1:16
- "In the beginning was the Word and the Word was with God, and the Word was God. . .the Word (Jesus) became flesh and dwelt among us." John. 1:1, 14
- "All things came into being through Him (Jesus); and apart from Him nothing came into being that has come into being." John 1:3

4. Mormon men say that the Father and the Son are separate Gods.

This denies the orthodox view of the Trinity. Mormons teach that Jesus Christ is a God named Jehovah, a different God from God the Father, whose name is Elohim.

- Bruce McConkie states: "Three separate personages—Father, Son, and Holy Ghost—comprise the Godhead...As *each of these persons is a God;* it is evident from this standpoint alone, that a *plurality of Gods* exists. To us...these *three are the only Gods* we worship" (*Mormon Doctrine*, p.576-7).
- James Talmage states: "This [the Trinity] *cannot rationally be construed to mean* that the Father, the Son and the Holy Ghost are one in substance and person" (*A Study of the Articles of Faith*, p.40).
- James Talmage states: *"Jesus Christ was Jehovah. . .*Jesus Christ, who is the Jehovah of the Old Testament. In all of scripture, where God is mentioned and where he has appeared, it was Jehovah. . .The Father has never dealt with man directly and personally since the fall" (Doctrines of Salvation, vol.1, p.11, 27).

- Joseph F. Smith stated, "Among the *spirit children* of Elohim, the first-born was and is *Jehovah, or Jesus Christ,* to whom all others are juniors" (*Gospel Doctrine*, p.70).

The Bible portrays Jesus as co-equal member of the Trinity.

Orthodox Christianity's established concept of God is that Jesus and the Father share the same essence (are one and the same God). A substantial part of the NT book of Colossians refutes the heresy of denying Christ's Deity.

5. **Mormon men say that Jesus is an elder brother who progressed to become a god**.

This is an attack on Jesus' person in that it lowers Him to our level and also raises us to His level.

- Milton R. Hunter: "*Jesus became a God* and reached His great state of understanding *through consistent effort and continuous obedience* to all the Gospel truths and universal laws" (*The Gospel Through the Ages*, p.51).
- Bruce McConkie states: "Christ the Word, the Firstborn, had of course *attained unto the status of Godhood* while yet in pre-existence" (*What Mormons Think of Christ*, p.36).
- Bruce McConkie claimed: "Jesus kept the commandments of his Father and thereby *worked out his own salvation,* and also set an example as to the way and the means whereby all men may be saved" (*The Mortal Messiah*, Vol.4, p.434).
- McConkie continues: "He [Jesus] is the Firstborn of the Father. *By obedience and devotion to the truth he attained* that pinnacle of intelligence which ranked him as a God, as the Lord Omnipotent, while yet in his pre-existent state" (*Mormon Doctrine*, p. 129).

The Bible states that Jesus has existed as God eternally. Here are a few of the many Bible verses that teach this.

- "In the *beginning was the Word*. . . the Word was God... the *Word became flesh* and dwelt among us." John 1:1, 14
- "But *of the Son* He (God) says, 'Thy Throne O God is *forever and ever.*'" Hebrews 1:8
- "Christ Jesus, who although *He existed* in the form of God, did not regard equality with God a thing to be grasped." Philippians 2:6
- "glorify me together with Thyself Father, with the glory which I ever had with Thee *before the world was.*" John 17:5
- "God. . .has in these last days spoken unto us by his Son, whom he hath appointed heir of all things, *by whom also he made the worlds.*" Hebrews 1:2

6. Mormon men say that Jesus Christ plays only an initial role in our salvation.

The previous teachings have been attacks on Christ's Person. This is an attack on the work of Christ. They say the work of Christ on the cross is **insufficient** for our complete salvation and men **must also perform works** in order to be fully saved.

- The *Book of Mormon* says of salvation: "for we know that it is by grace that we are saved, *after all that we can do*" (*Book of Mormon*, 2 Nephi 25:23).
- The Third Article of Faith states: "We believe that through the Atonement of Christ, all mankind may be saved, *by obedience to the laws and ordinances of the gospel*" (*Pearl of Great Price*: Articles of Faith).
- Joseph Fielding Smith explains what that last phrase means: "that which *man merits through his own acts* through life and by obedience to the laws and ordinances of the gospel" (*Doctrines of Salvation*, vol. 1, p.134).
- Spencer W. Kimball stated: "living *all the commandments guarantees total forgiveness of sins* and assures one of exalta-

tion. . . *trying is not sufficient. Nor is repentance* when one merely tries to abandon sin" (*The Miracle of Forgiveness*, p.164-165, 354-355).

The Bible clearly states that our complete salvation comes only through the finished work of Christ on the Cross, apart from any work on our part. One verse from the Bible sums up the problem with the Mormon concept of salvation:

- "For not knowing about God's righteousness, and *seeking to establish their own*, they did not subject themselves to the righteousness of God." Romans 10:3

The pronoun "they" in the verse above was directed at the Jews. But the truth applies as well to Mormons and to anyone who thinks he needs to add his efforts to the work of Christ. In contrast to Mormon leaders, in the New Testament the Apostle Paul clearly states the Gospel and salvation are without any works on our part. According to the Bible, our works are evidence and proof that we have salvation, but cannot help us <u>attain</u> salvation.

- "I do not frustrate the grace of God; *for if righteousness comes through the law, then Christ died needlessly."* Galatians 2:21
- "For by grace you have been saved through *faith*; and that *not of yourselves*, it is the gift of God; *not as a result of works that* no one should boast." Eph. 2:8-9
- "The *blood* of Jesus Christ his Son *cleanses us from all sin."* 1 John 1:7
- Paul responded to the Philippian jailor's question: "What must *I do* to be saved? **Believe** on the Lord Jesus Christ and you shall be saved." Acts 16:31
- The thief on the cross *did nothing but trust Him as Messiah and King*, but Jesus said to him, "Today you will be with me in Paradise." Luke 23:43
- Jesus: *"This is the work of God, that you believe on him* whom He (God the Father) has sent." John 5:29

- *"He saved us not on the basis of deeds which we have done in righteousness, but according to his mercy."* Titus 3:5
- "For Christ is the *end of the law for righteousness* to everyone who *believes."* Romans 10:4

7. Mormon men say that certain sins are beyond the atoning blood of Christ.

This is another attack on the work of Christ. It does two things. First, it lowers the value of His sacrifice for sins. Second, it elevates the value of man's blood to the level of being able to atone for sin.

- Brigham Young said: "It is true that the blood of the Son of God was shed for sins through the fall and those committed by men, yet *men can commit sins which it can never remit. . .there are sins that can be atoned for by an offering on the altar. . .and there are sins that the blood of a lamb. . .cannot remit,* but they *must be atoned for by the blood of the man"* (*Journal of Discourses*, vol.4, p.53-54, also published in Deseret News, p.235, 1856).
- Brigham Young said: "There is not a man or a woman, who violates the covenants [fidelity in marriage] made with their God, that will not be *required to pay the debt.* The *blood of Christ will never wipe that out, your own blood must atone for it"* (*Journal of Discourses,*vol.3, p.247)

According to this Mormon doctrine, there are certain sins which move the sinner beyond the forgiving power of the blood of Christ. The only way the sinner can get forgiveness is to have <u>his or her own blood</u> shed. This is really a misunderstanding of some Old Testament laws. In OT Israel certain crimes such as murder required the punishment of death. But the Law of Moses does not state that this punishment is the means of any forgiveness. In biblical terms, forgiveness always comes from God and cannot be earned even by spilling your own blood.

- Bruce McConkie explains: "But under certain circumstances there are some serious sins for which the *cleansing of Christ does not operate*, and the law of God is that *men must then have their own blood shed to atone* for their sins" (*Mormon Doctrine*, p.92).

- McConkie continues: "Christians speak often of the blood of Christ and its cleansing power. Much that is believed and taught on this subject, however, *is such utter nonsense and so palpably false that to believe it is to lose one's salvation.* Many go so far, for instance, as to pretend, at least, to believe that if we confess Christ with our lips and avow that we accept Him as our personal Savior, we are thereby saved. His blood, without other act than mere belief, they say, makes us clean" (*What the Mormons Think of Christ*, p.22).

- Joseph Fielding Smith (an LDS President) shows that this idea originated with Joseph Smith: "Joseph Smith taught that there were certain sins so grievous that man may commit, that they will place the transgressors *beyond the power of atonement of Christ.* If these offenses are committed, then the *blood of Christ will not cleanse* them from their sins even though they repent. Therefore their *only hope is to have their own blood shed to atone*, as far as possible, in their behalf" (Doctrines of Salvation, vol. 1, p.135); "the *law of sacrifice will have to be restored. . .*Sacrifice by the shedding of blood was instituted in the days of Adam and of necessity will have to be restored" (*Doctrines of Salvation*, vol. 3, p.94).

- Brigham Young said: "Will you love your brothers and sisters likewise, when they have *committed a sin that cannot be atoned for without the shedding of their own blood?. . .*This is loving our neighbor as ourselves; if he needs help, help him; and if he wants salvation and it is *necessary to spill his blood on the earth in order that he may be saved*, spill it" (*Journal of Discourses*, vol. 4, p.219-220).

The biblical teaching on blood atonement is that the shedding of blood is required for forgiveness of sin. However it is clear that it is the *blood of Christ* (Hebrews 9:22) that cleanses from *all sin*. (1 John 1:7)

The Bible teaches that Christ's sacrifice on the cross was complete for all time and eternity! We cannot add to it with our works:

- "He is able to *save forever* those who draw near to God through Him." Hebrews 7:25
- "He entered the holy place *once for all*, having obtained *eternal redemption*." Hebrews 9:12
- "So Christ also, having been *offered once* to bear the sins of many, shall appear." Hebrews 9:28.
- "He, having offered *one sacrifice for sins for all time. . .*" Hebrews 10:12
- "For by *one offering He has perfected for all time* those who are sanctified." Hebrews 10:14
- "There is *no longer any offering for sin*." Hebrews 10:18
- "Having forgiven us all our transgressions, having *cancelled out the certificate of debt. . .*He has *taken it out of the way*, having nailed it to the cross." Colossians 2:14.

8. Mormon men say that Jesus Christ is only one of many Saviors.

This goes back to Mormon Theology Proper. They believe that there are many universes. Our universe is only one of them. They believe that each universe has a god, earths, etc. This attacks the uniqueness of the biblical Jesus.

- According to Joseph Fielding Smith: "We are not the only people that the Lord has created. *We have brothers and sisters on other earths*. They look like us because they, too, are the children of God and were created in his image, for they are also his offspring" (*Mormon Doctrine* 1:62).
- Brigham Young taught: "Sin is upon every earth that ever was created . . . Consequently *every earth has its redeemer*,

and every earth has its tempter" (*Mormon Doctrine*, vol. 14, p.71).

The Bible states that Jesus Christ of Nazareth is the one and only Savior.

- Jesus claimed: *"I am THE way*, THE truth, and THE life; no one comes to the Father but by Me." John 14:6
- "For there is one God and *one mediator* also between God and men: the Man Christ Jesus." 1 Timothy 2:5
- "There is *salvation in no one else*; for there is *no other name under heaven* that has been given among men by which we must be saved." Acts 4:12

9. Mormon men say that Jesus was a polygamist.

This is an addition to the Scripture that is an attack on Jesus' person. It is an attack that lowers Jesus to the level of mere men.

Mormon prophets considered polygamy a righteous principle. They practiced it despite reversals in doctrine, and concessions to US Law by the LDS Church. They wanted to justify polygamy so they taught that Jesus was married and had multiple wives:

- Orson Pratt (LDS apostle) stated: "the great Messiah who was the founder of the Christian religion, *was a polygamist. . .marrying many honorable wives* himself...God the Father had a *plurality* of wives...the Son followed the example of his Father...both God the Father and our Lord Jesus Christ *inherit their wives* in eternity as well as in time" (*Mormon Doctrine*, p.172, 1853).
- Jedediah M. Grant (second counselor to Brigham Young) stated: "the burst of public sentiment in anathemas upon Christ and his disciples, *causing his crucifixion*, was evidently based on *polygamy...a belief of a plurality of wives caused the persecution of Jesus* and his followers" (*Mormon Doctrine*, vol. 1, p.346).

Some Mormon leaders contend that the wedding at Cana was an account of Jesus' marriage:

- Apostle Orson Hyde: "*...Jesus Christ was married at Cana of Galilee. . . Mary, Martha, and others were his wives . . .* he begat children." (*Journal of Discourses*, vol.2, p. 210)
- Jedediah M. Grant: *"Jesus was the bridegroom at the marriage of Cana* of Galilee, and he told them what to do. . . Now there was actually a marriage; and if Jesus was not the bridegroom on that occasion, please tell who was. If any man can show this, and prove that it was not the Savior of the world, then I will acknowledge I am in error. We say *it was Jesus Christ who was married,* to be brought into the relation whereby he could see his seed, before he was crucified." (*Journal of Discourses*, vol.6, p.345-346)
- Orson Hyde: "It will be borne in mind that once on a time, there was a marriage in Cana of Galilee; and on a careful reading of that transaction, it will be discovered that no less a person than *Jesus Christ was married on that occasion.* If he was never married, *his intimacy with Mary and Martha, and the other Mary* also whom Jesus loved, must have been highly unbecoming and improper to say the best of it." (*Journal of Discourses*, vol.2, p. 82-83)
- Orson Pratt: "We have now clearly shown that *God the Father had a plurality of wives,* one or more being in eternity, by whom He begat our spirits as well as the spirit of Jesus His First Born. . . We have also proved most clearly that the *Son followed the example of his Father, and became the great Bridegroom* to whom kings' daughters and many honorable wives are to be married." (*The Seer*, vol.1, 11, p. 169)

In contrast, the Bible says nothing about Jesus being married.

The Mormon interpretation of John 2 that says the Wedding in Cana was Jesus' own wedding ignores a reasonable, normal reading of the text:

- The Apostle John's stated purpose in describing the wedding feast at Cana was to recount Christ's first miracle (v. 11).
- According to John, Jesus and the disciples came because his mother Mary was invited (v.1). Why would Jesus or His mother need to be invited to Jesus' own wedding (v. 2)?
- Why is someone else referred to as the bridegroom (v. 9)?
- Why is there no mention of a physical wife or physical offspring for Jesus anywhere else in the Gospels or Epistles?

The fact that Jesus did not marry during His incarnation is consistent with the New Testament analogy that Jesus is the Bridegroom and the Church (collectively) is His spiritual bride.

- "For the husband is the head of the *wife,* as Christ also is head of the *church.* . .love your *wives,* just as Christ also loved the *church.* . .A man shall leave his father and mother and shall cleave to his wife; and the *two shall become one flesh.* This mystery is great, but *I am speaking with reference to Christ and the church.*" Ephesians 5:23-32
- The Bible describes an event called the "Marriage Supper" as that of the Lamb's marriage to the *Church, His bride* in Revelation 19:7; 21:2, 9.
- The Bible forbids polygamy.
- "Neither shall he [a leader of the people] multiply wives for himself, lest his heart turn away. . ." Deut 17:17

Jesus would not have been the perfect sacrifice if He had broken this command. The Bible teaches that Jesus was the spotless, sinless, perfect sacrifice for sinful men like us.

- ". . .but with precious blood, as of a lamb unblemished and spotless, the blood of Christ." 1 Peter 1:19
- ". . .how much more will the blood of Christ, Who through the eternal Spirit, offered Himself without blemish to God, cleanse your conscience from dead works to serve the living God." Hebrews 9:14

- "He made Him who knew no sin to be sin on our behalf, that we might become the righteousness of God in Him." 2 Corinthians 5:21

The Jesus of Mormonism is NOT the same person as the biblical Jesus!

The Bible gives severe warnings about twisting the truth about Jesus Christ and His message! One warning is in the New Testament book of Galatians:

"I am amazed that you are so quickly deserting Him who called you by the grace of Christ, for a different gospel, which is really not another (another of the same kind)...But even though we (Paul) or an angel from heaven, should preach to you a gospel contrary to that which we have preached to you, let him be accursed...If any man is preaching to you a Gospel contrary to that which you have received, let him be accursed." Galatians 1:6-9

Another warning is given by the Apostle John. He says,

"Who is the liar but the one who denies that Jesus is the Christ? This is the Antichrist, the one who denies the Father and the Son. Whoever denies the Son does not have the Father either; the one who confesses the Son has the Father also." I John 4:2-3

Where are the matching fingerprints? We can easily see the matching fingerprints if we categorize what we have learned. The first category has to do with Christ's Person (Who He is) and the second is Christ's Work (What He did). Mormons and Muslims assault both.

A matching fingerprint is the attack on the Person of Christ

Muslims say:

- Jesus was created, not eternal.
- Jesus was a slave, not King.
- Jesus is just a man, not God.
- Jesus was not resurrected.

Mormons say:

- Jesus was conceived by sexual intercourse, not born of a virgin.
- Jesus is the brother of Lucifer, not Lord over Lucifer.
- Jesus was first a spirit child, not eternally God.
- Jesus and the Father are separate gods, not one.
- Jesus was once a sinful man who progressed to become god.
- Jesus is only one of many Saviors, not unique.

A matching fingerprint is their attack on the Work of Christ

Muslims say:

- Jesus was not crucified, did not die on the Cross.
- Jesus prophesied the coming of Mohammed, was not preeminent.
- Salvation is found in the Five Pillars, NOT in Jesus.

Mormons say:

- Certain sins are beyond the atoning blood of Christ.
- Christ plays only an initial role in our salvation.

Chapter Conclusion

The biblical Jesus is neither the Islamic Jesus nor the Mormon Jesus. These distortions are Satan's attack on the person and the work of Jesus Christ.

The biblical Jesus is the true "Mighty God, Everlasting Father and Prince of Peace." Isaiah 9:6

Chapter 5

Questions for Discussion

1. What did Christ's pointed question teach the disciples?
2. What are the absolute fundamentals one must believe about Christ?
3. How would you respond to someone who believes that Jesus is Satan's brother?
4. How would you respond to the claim that there are many pathways to heaven?

Chapter 6

Detecting a Fingerprint Pattern in the Afterlife

Is Eternal Life Like a Box of Chocolates?

Why mention heaven? All religions except the religion of atheism believe in life after death. The Old Testament book of Ecclesiastes speaks to man's uncontrollable longing for transcendence, for meaning beyond this life. Ecclesiastes 3:11 says, "God has put eternity in the hearts of man." That verse tells us that because man is created (originally designed) to be rightly related to God, there is something that cries out for meaning beyond this life. Religion tries to fill that need. Muslims and Mormons believe in life after death.

The matching fingerprints here are these:

- Both Muslims and Mormons cannot be sure of entry into eternal bliss.
- Both Muslims and Mormons have layers or levels of eternal life.
- Both of the Muslim and Mormon heavens are man-centered and include sexual pleasure and/or procreation.

In dealing with the Mormon and Muslim views of eternal life, there are actually two questions. First, what will heaven be like for each religion? Then, can they be assured that they will have eternal life?

Let's begin with a popular quote from an American movie:

"My momma used to say, 'Life is like a box of chocolates. You never know what you are going to get.'" (Forrest Gump)

A common denominator between Muslims and Mormons is that both believe in life after death. When we dig a bit deeper we discover that they do not know what <u>kind</u> of eternal life they are going to get. We will see why for both groups, eternal life really is like a box of chocolates.

Muslim Paradise is Questionable

A Muslim can never be sure of possessing eternal life. But even if they could have the assurance that they are rightly related to Allah, they still are not sure what kind of eternal life they will get. This is because there are seven degrees, or levels, of Paradise. Muslims refer to their concept of heaven as "Paradise."

Muslim Paradise is an Oasis of Fleshly Gratification.

"Allah promiseth to the believers, men and women, Gardens underneath which rivers flow, wherein they will abide—blessed dwellings in Gardens of Eden. And—greater far!—acceptance from Allah." S 9:72

"A similitude of the Garden which those who keep their duty (to Allah) are promised: Therein are rivers of water unpolluted, and rivers of milk whereof the flavor changeth not, and rivers of wine delicious to the drinkers, and rivers of clear running honey; therein for them is every kind of fruit, with pardon from their Lord." S 47:15

". . .what of those on the right hand? Among thornless lote-trees, and clustered plantains, and spreading shade, and water gushing, and fruit in plenty neither out of reach nor yet forbidden, and raised couches; Of a rare creation have we created the Houris, and we have made them ever virgins, dear to their spouses, of equal age with them, for the people of the right hand." S 56:27-38

"....Allah has created the seven heavens one above another, and made the moon a light in their midst..." S. 71:15 and S. 67:1-3

The term "oasis" is a great description. It fits with Mohammed's homeland. His life revolved around Mecca and Medina in Saudi Arabia. These are desert places. There is a well in Mecca called the *Zam Zam* well. Muslims who are on their pilgrimage (*Hajj*) drink from this well. (According to some the water from this well has always been poor water.) Mohammed grew up in such a harsh desert environment. His view of heaven, then, would be the opposite of a harsh, dry, desert climate. He claimed that Paradise would include rivers of water, rivers of honey, rivers of wine. He taught that there would be no conserving and rationing of these resources. Each person can have all he wants. There are rivers of wine, rivers of honey, and rivers of milk. Muslim Paradise is an oasis!

The phrase "one of those on the right hand, among thornless lote-trees" indicates that there will be no hindrances. There will be no pain in gathering fruit. Mohammed's Paradise is a place of easy access to much fruit. The good stuff is easy to pick. This is a stark contrast to a desert environment. In Paradise there is fruit and plenty of it, neither out of reach nor forbidden. Also there are "raised couches." Mohammed grew up in tents. His Paradise is a life of comfortable ease in a desert oasis.

There is also a sensual side of their Paradise. According to Mohammed, there are some beautiful "beings" in Paradise that are specially created:

"We have created the *houris*, and have made them ever virgins, dear to their spouses, of equal age to them for the people of the right hand." S. 56:35-36

The "creations" mentioned above are called *houris*. The English word "whore" is derived from this Arabic word. These created beings are of equal age to the corresponding sexual partner in Paradise. They are "ever virgins." They are dear to their mates. The Qur'an says that they are soulless beings. The most significant aspect is that Muslim Paradise is sensual. It is filled with the creations (created beings) whose only purpose is to gratify fleshly desires.

The "people of the right hand" are followers of Allah. A Muslim doesn't use his left hand in the same way Westerners do. In some Islamic cultures, it is very offensive for you to pass or hand anything to someone else by using your left hand. The left hand is referred to as the "toilet hand" and is considered unclean.

Obviously, this description of Paradise is written from a man's perspective. The idea is that you lie on couches face to face and enjoy eternal sexual encounters with the *houris*. There are many descriptions of them in Islamic literature. Their eyes are large and are like pearls in shells. They are beautiful. Their breasts are even spoken of as "swelling." They are always equal in age to their assigned person. They are ever virgins in the sense of beauty and the implied sexual pleasure.

Paradise is a sensual oasis. It includes anything that your heart or body could desire. Mohammed was quoted as saying that devoted Muslim men who make it to Paradise will receive the power of a hundred men. They will be capable of sex at least one hundred times a day! In a nutshell, Muslim Paradise is a seven layered sensual or sexual oasis of relief, comfort, and shade.

Entry into Paradise is Based on Earthly Works.

Here are some key Qur'anic verses about entry into Paradise.

"Then those whose balance (of good deeds) is heavy,— they will attain salvation: But those whose balance is light, will be those who have lost their souls, in Hell will they abide." (Yusuf Ali's translation) S 23:102

"We shall set up scales of justice for the Day of Judgment, so that not a soul will be dealt with unjustly in the least, and if there be (no more than) the weight of a mustard seed, We will bring it (to account): and enough are We to take account." S 21:47

For Muslims, the works you do in the present life determine the rewards of Paradise. The quoted statements from the Qur'an refer to a balancing scale. On this scale, if your good deeds outweigh your bad deeds then you will go to Paradise. But if your bad deeds outweigh your good deeds you will go to hell. Accuracy is absolutely assured. The Surah says that even the weight of the mustard seed will be accounted for. Motives are included in calculating the weights. If you do a good deed with a bad motive, it will be counted as a bad deed. The idea is that the motive of your heart is just as important as the actions of your hands and feet. The terrible reality of this is that a Muslim can never know if his or her good works will outweigh the bad when they are measured.

Is there any way to guarantee entry into Paradise for a Muslim?

Only Martyrs are Guaranteed an Entry.

"Those who believe, and suffer exile and strive with might and main, in Allah's cause, with their goods and their persons, have the highest rank in the sight of Allah: they are the people who will achieve (salvation)." S 9:20

"I heard Allah's Apostle saying, 'The example of a Mujahid in Allah's Cause—and Allah *knows better who really strives in His Cause*—is like a person who fasts and prays continuously. *Allah guarantees that He will admit the Mujahid in His Cause into Paradise if he is killed*, otherwise He will return him to his home safely with rewards and war booty.'" *Sahih al-Bukhari*, Volume 4, Book 52, Number 46

There is only one way for a Muslim to be guaranteed eternal life in the highest Paradise. That way is the path of dying as a martyr. But even that isn't completely guaranteed because he does not know what level of heaven his reward will be. Even those who die in martyrdom still have a question mark on whether they will enter

Paradise. They say that only Allah knows the real motives of the heart. While we are unable to judge a person's motives, we can look at recent martyrs. Some of those who died as martyrs killing Israelis were paid handsomely. The checks were given to their families. The question is whether these martyrs died purely for the cause of Allah, or died so that their families would be taken care of with the money. What was their motive?

For a Muslim it is best to die in *jihad*. This could be death in battle or death for Allah as a suicide/homicide bomber. World news headlines are filled with reports of homicide bombers. For a Muslim, the surest and safest way to know what is in his "box of chocolates" is to die as a martyr. Even then, he is only casting himself upon Allah's will. Mohammed himself said,

> "By Allah, though I am the apostle of Allah, yet I do not know what Allah will do to me." (Hadith narrated by 'Um al 'Ala, vol. 5, book 58, #266)

Obviously, they have no security nor guarantee of what they are going to get. Eternal life for them is like the box of chocolates. They don't know if they will make it to Paradise, or to which of the seven levels they will go. That determination is based on their works and they never know if they have done enough works. Paradise is guaranteed only for martyrs.

On the other hand, Christians are assured of eternal life. I John 5:18 says, "these things have been written... that ye may KNOW that ye have eternal life"

Summary

Muslim Paradise:

- is sensual in nature
- involves seven levels
- is based on works
- is guaranteed only for martyrs.

Muslims simply do not have an anchor that offers any confident expectation.

Mormons Have Three Heavens.

All Pass Through the "Spirit World" First.

Mormon theology about life after death involves a time/place called "Spirit World." They believe that all humans exist first in a pre-mortal life. Following this, humans have a mortal life. Then there is a time in the "Spirit World." The Spirit World is a "place" where ALL people go when their physical life ends. It is not heaven; it is a kind of waiting period until heaven is determined for each person. After this phase humans enter "heaven." They are able to go to one of three different heavens. From highest to lowest those three levels are the Celestial Heaven, the Terrestrial Heaven and the Telestial Heaven.

Mormons believe that everyone must go through the Spirit World. A Mormon person's obedience and devotion to the LDS church is combined with how they progress in the Spirit World to determine which of the three heavens they enter.

Mormon Heaven has Three Levels

You could ask a Mormon, "If you died today, would you go to heaven?" In theory, an instructed Mormon person could say, "Yes." They could answer affirmatively, but they cannot know which heaven they are going to get. Like Muslims, for Mormons eternal life is like the box of chocolates. You never know what you are going to get until you get there. Or, until you "bite" into it. This is a perfect analogy to describe a Mormon's future. When a Mormon goes into the afterlife he doesn't know what he is going to get. There are three levels and each level is described differently.

Interestingly, the idea of three Mormon heavens comes from their book called *Doctrine and Covenants* and NOT from the *Book of Mormon*. This points back to a common denominator between Muslims and Mormons. The common denominator is that they both have a primary, key book that is followed by secondary books and writings. For Muslims it is the *Qur'an* and the *Hadith*. For Mormons it is the *Book of Mormon, Doctrine and Covenants,* and *Pearl of Great Price.*

The Mormon book that first teaches the idea of three heavens is *Doctrine and Covenants*. It says,

"A vision given to Joseph Smith the Prophet and Sidney Rigdon, at Hiram, Ohio, February 16, 1832." (*History of the Church* 1: 245 – 252)

Just before he instructed the Saints about the heavens, Joseph wrote,

"Upon my return from Amherst conference, I resumed the translation of the Scriptures. From sundry revelations which had been received, *it was apparent that many important points touching the salvation of man had been taken from the Bible, or lost before it was compiled.* It appeared self-evident from what truths were left, that if God rewarded every one according to the deeds done in the body, the term 'Heaven,' as intended for the Saints' eternal home, must include more kingdoms than one. Accordingly, while translating St. John's Gospel (John 5:29), myself and Elder Rigdon saw the following vision."

Entry to Highest Heaven Depends on Works

Joseph Smith taught that many important truths about salvation had been removed from the Bible by men or lost before it was compiled. He claimed that God has given him additional revelation. In view here is the new revelation that there are three different heavens. Mormons say that a person's assignment to a particular kingdom after death depends on that person's faith and works done in their mortal life.

Does that sound familiar? It reminds us of the Muslim point of view. Muslims also say that your destiny depends on your works. It is another common denominator. Both religions teach the concept that which kingdom/level you are assigned to after the resurrections depends on your works.

The Celestial Heaven is for only the most faithful Mormons. It is the ultimate Mormon heaven. Lesser to be desired is the Terrestrial heaven. The lowest Mormon heaven is Telestial. Telestial is supposedly much like life on earth only without pain.

Mormon Heavens are Sensual

Like Muslim Paradise, the Mormon Heaven is also a sensual place where sexual desires are gratified. Joseph Smith did not describe the pleasures as overtly as Mohammed. Perhaps Joseph knew that the American culture of his day would not tolerate such blatant and graphic descriptions. However, the sensual side is unmistakable in that men will be able to have sex with the wives who are sealed to them in Mormon temples. Joseph Smith teaches that there will be multiple sex partners but softens Mohammed's impact by making the partners wives instead of *houris*. The sexual unions are not only for pleasure. "Spirit children" are produced. Joseph simply made the sexual side of Mormon Heaven more tolerable for the western mindset. He was a smart man.

After Heaven, Exaltation

While it is not included as a heaven, there is an existence that is even higher than the Celestial Heaven. President Joseph Fielding Smith taught that the highest attainable degree is achieving godhood. This is called Exaltation. Mormons teach that if you serve faithfully in the celestial kingdom you may achieve Exaltation, which means you actually become a god!

Mormons teach that those in the Spirit World can continue to make progress toward their assignment to a higher heaven. Mormons believe that all men, not just Mormons, go to the Spirit World. Joseph had to invent some way for the people who died before the Gospel was restored to the earth in the 1830's to get to a heaven. He taught that those who believe the restored Mormon gospel can help those who died without believing it. The help that living Mormons give dead non-Mormon people is known as "Baptism for the Dead" or "Proxy Baptism." Living devout Mormons can help people progress in the afterlife by being baptized for them. The secret of successfully helping a departed person make progress is being an obedient and devoted Mormon yourself. This eternal progression is Joseph's own curious and creative invention.

Outer Darkness

Mormons also teach that those who commit the unpardonable sin of rejecting the restoration of the gospel through Joseph Smith do not inherit any degree of glory whatsoever. They are resurrected and reside in a state called "outer darkness." The ones who receive no kingdom of glory but go to "outer darkness" instead are known as the "sons of Perdition." These would be people who actively teach against the LDS church or who simply reject Mormon doctrine.

Summary

For Mormons, assignment to a particular kingdom in the afterlife depends on an individual's faith and works done during mortal life and the spirit world.

Chapter Conclusion

These are the matching fingerprints on the Mormon and Muslim afterlife:

- Neither can be sure of entry into eternal life.
- Both have varying levels of heaven.
- Both heavens are man-centered and sensual.
- Entry into the greatest reward depends on your works.

Each perverts how the Bible describes Heaven.

Chapter 6

Questions for Discussion

1. Does being assured of Heaven allow freedom to sin? Why? Why not?
2. How can the biblical Heaven be a joyous place when some are not there?
3. Does the biblical Heaven include family life? Defend your answer.

Chapter 7

Profiling Women for Matching Fingerprints

Pregnant Virgins?!

Wow! Is this a hot-potato topic for our day! This information could be ammunition for the radical feminists whom Rush Limbaugh, a conservative American talk radio host, refers to as "femi-nazis." Interestingly, radical feminists should be up in arms against the Mormon and Muslim views regarding male and female equality. They should be shouting at the top of their lungs over this issue!

Simply stated, the **matching fingerprint is that both Muslim and Mormon theology see women as second class citizens.** Treating women as second class citizens is unacceptable on several levels. The greatest evil is that it hinders key relationships of life. In particular it hurts the husband-wife relationship. According to these two religions, women will be either eternally pregnant or eternally losing their virginity. Either way women are lowered to the level of a second class companion who serves as a sex partner.

Why is Satan pleased with religious belief that destroys the relationship between men and women? Because Satan always wants to destroy harmonious relationships! It is his calling card. Relationship is the foundation of the universe. The first relationship was and is between the Father, the Son, and the Holy Spirit—the Christian

Trinity. Before there was a material universe, there was relationship! Satan hates it because it is God's plan. He seeks to destroy personal relationships.

On a spiritual level, destroying the relationship between man and wife damages the great biblical analogy of Christ and His Bride, the Church.

In Genesis we see that both Adam and Eve were created for a relationship. Adam was to walk in harmony with God. But Adam needed Eve's companionship. She was created because "it is not good for man to be alone." Eve "completed" the relationship with Adam. If the woman is viewed as inferior a barrier is placed between husband and wife. This view refuses to accept the biblical idea that men and women are equal.

Christian Thought about Women's Issues

Before we get to the Muslim and Mormon views, let's take a look at the biblical view. The biblical concept regarding women can be found in Galatians 3:26-28:

> "For you are all sons of God through faith in Christ Jesus. For all of you who were baptized into Christ have clothed yourselves with Christ. There is neither Jew nor Greek, there is neither slave nor free man, **there is neither male nor female**; for you are all one in Christ Jesus."

1. Equality of the Sexes

The Christian view of women and men is that they are EQUAL IN VALUE! The verse teaches that cultural (slave/free) and racial (Jew/Gentile) barriers are removed in Christ. In the same way, barriers between men and women are removed. Men and women are not to see each other as superior and/or inferior. Equality is the idea. Christians should not make distinctions between male and female in terms of value. Women and men are equally valuable to God.

2. Roles are Assigned

However, we must also keep in mind that God has ordained specific roles for both men and women. The roles include those who are to lead and those who are to follow. But the leader/follower roles do NOT mean there is inequality. First Corinthians 11:3 gives insight into this:

> "But I want you to understand that Christ is the head of every man, and the man is the head of a woman, and God is the head of Christ."

Notice that this verse teaches that Jesus Christ assumes a role. Christ is equal with God the Father, but God the Father is the head of Christ. In same way, the head of woman is man. Headship has nothing to do with value or usefulness or intelligence. It has to do only with role. This order of roles reflects God's creation. The Christian view is that men and women are equal in value but have different roles that reflect God's creation and order.

3. Weaker Vessels

Another passage is I Peter 3:7:

> "You husbands likewise, live with your wives in an understanding way, as with a weaker vessel, since she is a woman; and grant her honor as a fellow-heir of the grace of life, so that your prayers may not be hindered."

This verse teaches that men ought to take care of and treat women as if they are "weaker." Do not be confused by *weaker*. This is not "weak" in the sense of strength or value. The word is used in the sense of something *precious, fine and fragile*. Men care for what they deem precious. It may be a beloved car, trophy, tool, or musical instrument. The care we give that treasured object is the kind of care we each should give our wife. This is part of the biblical Christian view of the sexes.

Muslim Thought about Women's Issues

The sad state of women's rights in Muslim countries is well documented. One such book is *Voices Behind the Veil* by Dr. Ergun Caner. In this book Dr. Caner is the general editor of various articles about women's issues written by others. Several of the chapters are by people who could not identify themselves because of personal safety concerns. Speaking out against the Muslim doctrine or practice is always dangerous.

Another book is *The Price of Honor* by Jan Goodwin. This book is not written from a Christian perspective. It is subtitled, "Muslim women lift the veil of silence on the Islamic world." It is a New York Times notable book. It is very interesting to see a non-Christian view of women's issues in Islamic countries. Even non-Christians take notice of this problem. More should be said!

At a high point of Islamic cultural influence a Muslim scholar named Al-Ghazali (1058-1111 AD) catalogued a list of 18 ways in which women are inferior to men. We will not look at all 18 of them. However, the following issues are included in Al-Ghazali's list. These are intelligence, marriage, polygamy, spirituality, sexuality, inheritance and physical abuse.

1. Inequality of Intelligence

The Muslim view is that women are not as intelligent as men. This shows up in a legal setting. To strict Muslims the testimony of a woman in a court or legal case is worth only half the testimony as a man because the female mind is considered deficient. Sura 2 describes how financial transactions should be written down and witnessed. Part of section 282 says,

> "Let his guardian dictate faithfully, and get two witnesses, out of your own men, and if there are not two men, then a man and two women, such as ye choose, for witnesses, so that if one of them errs, the other can remind her. The witnesses should not refuse when they are called on."

The unmistakable implication is that women are not as reliable as men when it comes to serving as witnesses. We can couple Surah 2:282 with a Hadith to get a fuller picture of the Muslim view:

"The Prophet said, 'Isn't the witness of a woman equal to half of that of a man?'" The women said, "Yes." He said, "This is because of the deficiency of a woman's mind." (Hadith narrated by Abu Said Al-Khudri, 3:826)

Mohammed was kind enough to allow some women to ask him about their intellectual deficiencies. His response tells us more of how he felt about women. Mohammed said:

"O womenfolk, you should give charity and ask much forgiveness for I saw you in bulk amongst the dwellers of Hell. A wise lady among them said: Why is it, Messenger of Allah that our folk are in bulk in Hell? Upon this the Holy Prophet observed: You curse too much and are ungrateful to your spouses. I have seen none lacking in common sense and failing in religion but (at the same time) robbing the wisdom of the wise, besides you. Upon this the woman remarked: What is wrong with our common sense and with religion? He (the Holy Prophet) observed: Your lack of common sense (can be well judged from the fact) that the evidence of two women is equal to one man, that is a proof of the lack of common sense." (*Sahih Muslim*, Abdul Hamid Siddiqi, tr., Number 142.)

Please notice that at first Mohammed justifies his claim that women lack common sense by reminding them that their testimony is worth half that of a man. In the second reference Mohammed justifies his claim that the testimony of women is half as good as men's testimony, by stating that women have deficient minds! What a classic example of *circular reasoning!*

2. Marriage and Divorce Rights

A second area has to do with marriage and divorce. A Muslim man can look at a wife and say, "I divorce you," three times, and that is as good as being divorced. But can a woman do that? No way! The woman is without recourse in such situations. The woman is bound by the man's pronouncement.

Marriage is a MUST for Muslim women. A woman's entry into Paradise is tied to her being both married and in a pleasing relationship with her husband. The Qur'an teaches that if a woman dies while her husband is not pleased with her she will not be able to enter Paradise. Allah will refuse her entrance. They are basically saying, "If you get run over by a camel and die while you are not rightly related to your husband, even if he is just mad at you, you will not go to Paradise." The key idea about marriage and divorce is that the power lies in the hands of the man. The woman is powerless.

3. Polygamy

Islamic polygamy also points to viewing women as inferior to men. A Muslim man is allowed to have four wives. A Muslim man has all the cards. In some cultures he can forsake a wife at any time and for almost any reason. A Muslim woman does not have the same option. According to the *Hadith,* Mohammed taught that four wives was a good number. Some speculate that four is the usual number of wives because there are four weeks in a month. Islam forbids sexual contact with a woman in her menstrual cycle. If a man has four wives it is more likely that one will always be available for sex. It sounds crass and selfish but the idea is that the man can always count on his sexual desire being fulfilled. So, four was the number of wives for a man. Remember that marriage is a must for a Muslim woman. Qur'anic thought assumes that a woman will have a husband.

Sura 33:50 is a long verse that gives Mohammed wide latitude in his polygamous marriages. It seems that Mohammed had special permissions from Allah to violate the rules that were given to others. He was married many times and had numerous additional partners. Sura 33:50 says,

"O Prophet, We have made lawful to you those of your wives, whose dowers you have paid, and those women who come into your possession out of the slave-girls granted by Allah, and the daughters of your paternal uncles and aunts, and of your maternal uncles and aunts, who have migrated with you, and the believing woman who gives herself to the Prophet, if the Prophet may desire her."

4. Spirituality

Muslims teach that women are to "abandon prayer" during their menstrual cycle. A menstruating woman is not allowed to recite the Qur'an. In Islamic culture, a woman's spirituality is put on hold when she is in her menstrual cycle. Mohammed taught that this was a time of ritual uncleanness and she is not allowed to go to prayer. This is an attack on something that the female is absolutely unable to control. It is another way that women are put down as second class citizens. A woman is helplessly unspiritual at some times.

In contrast, the New Testament says nothing about a ritual uncleanness because of menstruation. The Scripture encourages all believers, male and female, to "pray without ceasing" (1 Thessalonians 5:17-18) and "pray always" (Ephesians 6:18). With Christians there is no time of the month when a lady cannot enter God's presence in prayer and worship.

5. Sexuality and Dress

All of us have seen photos of how some Islamic cultures require women to dress. Simply stated, they are not allowed much freedom in public dress style. It seems that Mohammed was strongly sexual and apparently could not keep his mind clear of lustful images. He responded to this by requiring women to dress in a way that covered everything. There are many rules about dress, and Islamic women bear the brunt and burden of the regulations. The Islamic view is that they wear veils on earth to protect men from being tempted with lustful thoughts.

In Paradise the opposite is true. In Paradise men seem to have the ability to see through their clothes. The Qur'an teaches that in Paradise, even if a woman wears seventy layers of clothing, men will be able to peer through and see the "marrow of her legs." On earth they have to wear veils and *burquas*. In Paradise they are the objects of men's eyes. Their husbands (and apparently all men) will be able to see right through their clothes. They have no choice about wearing a veil here, and they have no choice about being on display in Paradise. Women are powerless and suffer the extremes.

For Muslims sexual freedom is a man's right but not a woman's right. The general Muslim belief is that sexual enjoyment is primarily for men and not women. One plain example is a husband's attitude toward sex. A husband has sex with his wife, as a plow goes into a dirt field. Sura 2:223 says,

"Your women are your fields, so go into your fields which-ever way you like . . . "

Please do not overlook the plain analogy of this verse. It alludes to women as possessions (like a field). More explicitly, it includes sexual positions and practices. A Muslim man may plow his field as he wishes. The Hadiths are very explicit about sexual conduct. In general the Muslim husband has absolute control over their sex life. If a woman does not want to have sex, then angels curse her.

Remember that the Hadiths are the records of Mohammed's words and actions. They are not the Qur'an but are seen as authoritative for belief and practice. The most reliable Hadith collector Bukhari says:

"If a man invites his wife to sleep with him and she refuses to come to him, then the angels send their curses on her till morning."

Another facet of sexuality that tilts in favor of men is this: Muslim men were allowed to have sex with women who were taken as captives. Again, the man and his pleasure are in focus in this religion. Women are clearly second-rate.

6. Inheritance Rights

The Qur'an gives guidelines about distributing an inheritance after a person dies. When it comes to how women are viewed, Sura 4:11 says,

"Allah directs you in regard to your children's inheritance. To the male, a portion equal to that of two females."

Since inheritance usually involved land ownership, there may be a practical and cultural aspect to this because men are the ones that provide for their families. However, the inference is that women are only half as valuable as men even in receiving an inheritance. Again, women are lower than men.

7. Physical Abuse

A Muslim husband may hit his wife/wives if he even suspects "highhandedness" in a wife. This gives the man a wide power to judge his wife's motives and actions. The clear idea is that domestic violence is acceptable!
In Sura 4:34, The Qur'an says:

". . . If you fear highhandedness from your wives, remind them [of the teaching of God], then ignore them when you go to bed, then hit them. If they obey you, you have no right to act against them. God is most high and great."

A *Hadith* says that Muslim women in the time of Mohammed were suffering from domestic violence.

"Rifa'a divorced his wife whereupon 'AbdurRahman bin Az-Zubair Al-Qurazi married her. 'Aisha said that the lady (came), wearing a green veil and complained to her (Aisha) of her husband and showed her a green spot on her skin caused by beating. It was the habit of ladies to support each other, so when Allah's Apostle came, 'Aisha said, "I have not seen any woman suffering as much as the believing women. Look! Her skin is greener than her clothes!" (Bukarhi)

In Sura 4:34, the Qur'an teaches that if a wife doesn't listen to her husband, then the husband should admonish her. If that does not work then he should make her sleep in a separate bed. If the wife still does not respect her husband's authority, even after she has been banished to another bed, the husband is told to physically punish her.

Much more could be written about the Muslim view of women. However this book is not meant to be exhaustive. Our intent is only to compare the Muslim and Mormon views and look for matching fingerprints. Let us now turn our attention to the Mormon view.

Mormon Thought about Women's Issues

It is inescapable. Much of the Mormon view mirrors the Muslim view of women and women's issues. It seems clear that Joseph Smith was brilliant at fashioning some of Mohammed's ideas into more acceptable language for his day. Satan's fingerprints match! Much more could be written, but for now examine four areas of Mormon thought about women. These four areas match Muslim thought. They are inequality with men, marriage, polygamy, and sexuality.

1. Inequality with men

It sounds shocking to say, but in truth Mormon women are not considered equal to Mormon men. Consider the leadership structure of the Mormon Church.

There are NO WOMEN in the leadership structure of the church. In fact, most leadership emphasis is on men. All Mormon men are ordained as members of the "priesthood" with the absolute authority to preach the gospel, bestow blessings, prophecy, perform healings and baptisms, and generally speak for God.

James H. Snowden says,

"Their priesthood gives them the right to advise and instruct the Saints (i.e., Mormons), and their jurisdiction extends over all things spiritual and temporal" (*The Truth About Mormonism,* page 134).

At age twelve, Mormon boys become members of the Aaronic, or lesser priesthood, and at nineteen become eligible for the Melchezedek, or higher priesthood. Members of either priesthood are elevated. They are given higher spiritual authority than those who are not priests. Please note two things about this priesthood. First, *women are excluded from the priesthood.* Second, this practice, in effect, says that a woman's twelve year old son is more qualified to advise her in spiritual matters than she is to advise him. A Mormon insider, Sonia Johnson, says that the official explanation is that women are kept from having the priesthood because women are more spiritual than men, therefore, men need to have the priesthood to teach them how to be better people (*From Housewife to Heretic,* page 86). Women are also told that because they have the all-important ability to bear children, men need the power of the priesthood merely to remain equal with them. Sounds fishy!

2. Mormon Marriage

All Mormon women must be married in order to go to the highest heaven. Mormon women today are still brought up to believe that the most important thing they can do is "to marry the right person, in the right place, by the right authority" (*Mormon Doctrine* by Bruce R. McConkie, page 118). Deborah Laake, who was excommunicated in 1993 for writing *Secret Ceremonies: A Mormon Woman's Intimate Diary*, states that "it had been repeatedly impressed on me that if I failed to marry a faithful Mormon man. . .in a Mormon temple, I would be denied access to the highest level of Mormon heaven." Being married in a temple was also ingrained into her thinking. She was taught that the temple marriage is so important "that a longing for romance on earth should not be allowed to interfere with it."

Mormons are taught that marriage and family are forever. As noted earlier, if you see a bumper sticker that says, "Families Are Forever," it is usually on a car owned by a Mormon.

Mormon young people are taught that a good and proper Mormon home is a patriarchal one. A handbook written for fourteen year old boys states that, "The patriarchal order is of divine origin and will continue throughout time and eternity." Husbands conduct family prayers, bless their wives and children, and generally control the household. They also are in charge of "family home evening," one night per week set aside for family prayer and togetherness. The Mormon belief is that Eve's roles in life, those of helpmeet and childbearer, set the pattern for all of her daughters (*Mormon Doctrine*, page 844). Girls are told that God wants them at home.

For a Mormon man to receive the highest heavenly reward, he must be "married for eternity" in the Mormon temple. This special marriage is binding both before and after death. As it relates to women, this "Celestial" marriage is essential. Without being celestially married to a holder of the priesthood, a woman cannot be "saved."

Mary Ettie Smith, a Mormon woman who left the church and Utah in 1856, said that "women do not amount to much in themselves," and that women in those times were often celestially married to men they had no intention of ever living with, so that they could have a man who would be able to get them into heaven. (*Mormonism: Its Rise, Progress and Present Condition,* N. W. Green, p. 154).

In the temple marriage ceremony women are given secret names known only to their husbands. These secret names are for identification so their husbands can pull them through to "the other side" after death. Historically, during the marriage ceremony men made their temple covenants directly to God, while the women had to make their temple covenants to their husbands. This means that while male temple workers, representing God, led the men through the cloth representing the veil between worlds, husbands symbolically led their wives through. Women also promise to obey their husbands in everything as long as their husbands obey God. As part of the ceremony women also receive their endowments. Endowments are sacred ordinances and promises which make a person eligible to enter the highest level of heaven. Marriage is vital to a Mormon woman who is concerned about the after-life.

After death, while their husbands are creating and ruling over planets, the women have the questionable honor of bearing his "spirit children" for eternity. These spirit children descend to their father's planet to inhabit bodies as mortals, who are then ruled over by him. *Mormon Doctrine* states that these celestially married men and women "will live eternally in the family unit and have spirit children, thus becoming Eternal Fathers and Eternal Mothers." A man who has multiple wives can beget many more spirit children, making him much more powerful. Mormon men must beget as many children with as many wives as possible, for "their glory (in heaven) is in proportion to the number of their wives and children" (Snowden 141). Some Mormon men I knew in Utah often commented on how much they looked forward to this part of heaven. It was not inappropriate or crude. It is simply their theology.

3. Polygamy

In 1843, Joseph Smith, the founder of the Mormon Church, announced to the press that despite rumors to the contrary the Latter-day Saints did not practice polygamy and believed it was an abomination. He spoke the truth as far as the vast majority of Mormons was concerned, for polygamy is expressly forbidden in the Book of Mormon. The Book of Jacob (in the Book of Mormon) says,

"24 Behold, David and Solomon truly had many wives and concubines, which thing was abominable before me, saith the Lord. 25 Wherefore, thus saith the Lord, I have led this people forth out of the land of Jerusalem, by the power of mine arm, that I might raise up unto me a righteous branch from the fruit of the loins of Joseph. 26 Wherefore, I the Lord God will not suffer that this people shall do like unto them of old. 27 Wherefore, my brethren, hear me, and hearken to the word of the Lord: For there shall not any man among you have save it be one wife; and concubines he shall have none; 28 For I, the Lord God, delight in the chastity of women.

And whoredoms are an abomination before me; thus saith the Lord of Hosts. 29 Wherefore, this people shall keep my commandments, saith the Lord of Hosts, or cursed be the land for their sakes." (Book of Jacob 2:24-29)

However Joseph himself had been married to at least eleven women besides his legal wife by 1843. The first of these, in 1835, was a seventeen year old orphan who had been taken in by his wife, Emma Smith. Joseph married some of these women without the knowledge of either his wife or his fellow Mormons.

On July 12, 1843, Joseph Smith declared that God had given him a new revelation concerning marriage. He revealed it to his brother and other high-ranking male church members. This "revelation" from God named Joseph's wife specifically. It instructed "mine handmaid Emma Smith, Joseph's wife" to accept this doctrine and allow Joseph to have as many wives as he liked, as long as they were all "virtuous and pure." (*The Truth about Mormonism,* James H Snowden, p. 191)

Emma Smith was a very strong-willed woman. It is reasonable to believe that Joseph was frightened of her wrath. He sent his brother, Hyrum, to inform her of God's plan. Emma was understandably scornful, and reportedly threw Hyrum out of her house. Later she managed to obtain a written copy of the revelation, and while in Joseph's presence, tossed it directly into the fireplace. But the damage had already been done. Joseph is said to have been married to twenty-seven wives at the time of his death! Emma left the church after his death and later denied that her husband had ever practiced polygamy (*The Twenty-Seventh Wife,* by Irving Wallace, page 65).

Among the reasons given for the practice of polygamy, the most popular was that God had commanded it through Joseph Smith. We must remember that Joseph claimed to be the living prophet of God. This is also Mohammed's pattern. Joseph and other LDS "prophets" taught that polygamy is holy and was practiced commonly in ancient times until people began spreading false religions. Adam, in his previous, spiritual existence, had many wives, of whom Eve was just one. Mormons taught that Jesus was also a polygamist who was married and saw His seed before He was crucified. Mormons taught that his wives were Mary, Martha, and Mary Magdalene. *Mormon Doctrine* states that the president of the church had to suspend the practice of polygamy in 1890 because of the conditions at the time, but "obviously the holy practice will commence again after the Second Coming. . ." *(Mormon Doctrine*, page 578).

Polygamous marriage is essential to Mormon theology. *Mormon Doctrine* states that God was once a man, and "He is now a glorified, resurrected Personage having a tangible body of flesh and bones" (page 250). Mormons believe that all of the gods first existed as spirits, then came to an earth to receive bodies. Then after having passed through a period of probation on their earth, they were advanced to the exalted position of godhood. After death, a good Mormon man who has been obedient and devoted is catapulted to this same status and receives his own planet to populate and rule over. To receive this honor, a man must be "married for eternity" in the Mormon temple.

4. Sexuality

Mormon men are the focus when it comes to physical relationships with their wives both on earth and as part of their heavenly reward. Joseph Smith sets the tone for an attitude toward sex in the earthly life.

Smith's close friend and First Councilor, William Lay says, "Joseph was very free in his talk about his women. He told me one day of a certain girl and remarked that she had given him more pleasure than any girl he had ever enjoyed. I told him it was horrible to talk like this." (William Law, Interview in *Salt Lake Tribune*, July 31, 1887).

Mormon Apostle Hebert Kimball says, "I have noticed that a man who has but one wife, and is inclined to that doctrine, soon begins to wither and dry up, while a man who goes into plurality [polygamy] looks fresh, young, and sprightly." (*Journal of Discourses* Vol 5, page 22) Kimball also says, "I think no more of taking another wife than I do of buying a cow." (*The Twenty Seventh Wife*, Irving Wallace, p. 101)

The Mormon concept of heaven includes sexual activity with multiple wife-partners. This heavenly sex keeps the eternal wives eternally pregnant. The tone always centers around the man. The point of sex seems to be the man's pleasure and the increase of his physical offspring on earth and spiritual offspring in the afterlife.

The matching fingerprint between Muslims and Mormons in this area is that sexuality is a man's delight instead of being something mutually enjoyed by both sexes.

We can see specific matching fingerprints concerning women's issues if we categorize what we have learned.

A matching fingerprint is inequality with men.

Muslims say:

- Women are not allowed in leadership positions.
- Women's inheritance is less than a man's.
- Women's intelligence is less than a man's.

Mormons say:

- Women are not allowed in leadership

A matching fingerprint is marriage.

Muslims say:

- Women are powerless in divorce.
- Women must marry to go to highest Paradise.
- Women must please husband to avoid spiritual judgment.

Mormons say:

- Women must marry to go to highest Heaven.
- Women will be married in eternity.

A matching fingerprint is polygamy and sexuality.

Muslims say:

- Women have no sexual freedom.
- Sexual enjoyment is primarily for men.
- Women must accept polygamy.
- Women's dress is strict to prevent sexual temptation.

Mormons say:

- Women have no sexual freedom.
- Sexual enjoyment is primarily for men
- Women will live with polygamy in eternity.

A matching fingerprint is spirituality.

Muslims say:

- Women are spiritually unclean in the menstrual cycle.
- Women will not enter Paradise if they are not pleasing to their husbands.

Mormons say:

- Women do not receive a spiritual priesthood

Chapter Conclusion

The fingerprints on the Mormon and Muslim views on women's issues match. Both reduce women to second-class citizens in this life *and* in the afterlife. This is a great evil that accomplishes Satan's purpose of ruining some of life's most meaningful relationships.

Chapter 7

Questions for Discussion

1. What are the hot topic women's issues of our present day?
2. How does the Bible address these issues? Defend your answers.
3. How would being a "second class citizen" affect everyday life for women?

Chapter 8

Contaminating the Evidence About Israel

Do They Replace Israel as God's Chosen People?

Mormons, Muslims, Christians and Jews alike claim to be the physical and/or spiritual descendants of Abraham. Abraham is our starting point. When God called Abram out of polytheistic paganism He gave Abram great promises. One of those promises is:

> "And I will bless them that bless thee, and curse him that curseth thee: and in thee shall all families of the earth be blessed. (Genesis 12:3)"

A promise of blessing goes to those who support and bless the descendants of Abram (later called Abraham). Mormons, Muslims, Christians and Jews all want to be recognized as Abraham's children.

The name Israel refers to ethnic Hebrews as well as the political nation that exists in the Middle East. In this chapter we will see that it is important for Christians to support Israel. We will then see the matching fingerprint that both Muslims and Mormons claim to be replacements for Israel.

Since the common view is that they believe they replace Israel, we must understand "replacement." This teaching is known as Replacement Theology. We will seek to understand Replacement Theology before moving to the specifics of what Muslims and Mormons believe. We begin with the general idea that the nation Israel has a right to exist.

A Biblical Perspective of Israel

Christians have many reasons to appreciate and support Israel.

• The Bible teaches us to bless the Jews.

> "And I will bless them that bless thee, and curse him that curseth thee: and in thee shall all families of the earth be blessed." Genesis 12:3
>
> "Let people serve thee, and nations bow down to thee: be lord over thy brethren, and let thy mother's sons bow down to thee: cursed be every one that curseth thee, and blessed be he that blesseth thee." Genesis 27:29
>
> "Blessed is he that blesseth thee, and cursed is he that curseth thee." Numbers 24:9

• The Jews gave us the Bible.

> "What advantage then hath the Jew? Or what profit is there of circumcision? Much every way: chiefly, because that unto them were committed the oracles of God." Romans 3:1-2

• Christians are part of God's New Covenant with Israel.

> "Behold, the days come, saith the LORD, that I will make a new covenant with the house of Israel, and with the house of Judah…" Jeremiah 31:31
>
> "I will make a new covenant with the house of Israel and with the house of Judah: Not according to the cove-

nant that I made with their fathers. . .A new covenant, he hath made. . ." Hebrews 8:8-13.

• Satan hates the Jews.

He has always wanted to destroy them and cut off the lineage of the Messiah.

> "And Satan stood up against Israel, and provoked David to number Israel." 1Chronicles 21:1
>
> "And when the dragon saw that he was cast unto the earth, he persecuted the woman (Israel) which brought forth the man child (Jesus)." Revelation 12:13

We should stand for Israel because our enemy, Satan, is against her. Standing against Satan's desire is reason enough.

• Our Messiah is Jewish!

Jesus is not a white man. He is not a black man. He is not Hispanic or Native American. He is Jewish. Jesus is an Israeli! The Bible teaches that Jesus is of the seed of Abraham, of the tribe of Judah, and of the lineage of David.

> "And in thy (Abraham) seed shall all the nations of the earth be blessed (by Messiah); because thou hast obeyed my voice." Genesis 22:18
>
> "The book of the generation of Jesus Christ, the son of David, the son of Abraham. . ." Matthew 1:1
>
> "The scepter shall not depart from Judah, nor a lawgiver from between his feet, until Shiloh come; and unto him shall the gathering of the people be." Genesis 49:10
>
> "For it is evident that our Lord sprang out of Judah; of which tribe Moses spake nothing concerning priesthood." Hebrews 7:14

"For unto us a child is born, unto us a son is given. .
.Of the increase of his government and peace there shall
be no end, upon the throne of David. . ."Is 9:6-7

"And when Jesus departed thence, two blind men
followed him, crying, and saying, Thou Son of David,
have mercy on us." Matthew 9:27

Why a Nation Israel

Some might say, "Wait. The fact that Jesus was an Israeli does
not mean that we should respect the political nation of Israel now,
two thousand years later." On the surface that statement seems to
have merit. However, if you look closely at the texts mentioned
above, you will observe that Jesus will ALWAYS be an Israeli and
some form of the nation will always exist.

Make no mistake, Christians are NOT called upon to offer a
blanket endorsement of Israel which might include extreme acts such
as violations of human rights. However Christians should support
Israel's right to exist as a race of people as well as a political nation.
To deny that Israel should exist is to deny something the Bible takes
for granted. This makes it anti-biblical to be anti-Semitic.

In contrast, some of the nations surrounding Israel have vowed to
push her into the sea. They intend to absolutely annihilate the entire
nation. For example, if you find a photo of Yasir Arafat in his olive
drab PLO uniform and look closely at the patch on his shoulder, you
will see a map of the Middle East. Look closely and you will see that
there is no nation of Israel on that map. The symbolism is obvious.

God has a plan for the nation of Israel. He is not finished with
her.

God's Future Plan for Israel

Mentioning God's future design for the nation of Israel often
starts a heated discussion among Christians. Some Christians believe
that God has abandoned his plan and promises to Israel and has
transferred them to the New Testament Church.

Others see the New Testament Church as a parenthesis in God's
overall design. This parenthesis is called "the Church Age." It is a

mystery in the Old Testament that is revealed in the New Testament. They believe that after the parenthesis, God's focus will shift back to Israel. These people are called Dispensationalists.

The Bible Timeline

"Dispensationalism" comes from the Greek word that means "house rule" as used in Ephesians 1:10 and 3:2. It is a way of looking at biblical history. It is rooted in an obvious fact: God has "ruled His house" in different ways in different times. In the Old Testament God worked with His people Israel through a sacrificial system. In the New Testament following the death of Jesus, He changed the way He works with men.

We all agree that there is an Old Testament and a New Testament. We all agree that there is a difference in how God worked in the Old and New Testaments. Agreeing that there is a difference makes everyone somewhat of a dispensationalist!

Figurative or Literal?

Dispensationalists consistently use a literal hermeneutic. A literal hermeneutic is a plain, normal interpretation of Scripture. When the literal interpretation makes sense, we do not seek to impose another meaning on a biblical text. When a text says that there will be a day in which a lion lies down beside a lamb and that children will be able to play with poisonous snakes without fear, we interpret that literally. It will happen!

We can see the importance of the literal interpretation when we look at Christ's First and Second Comings. The First Coming (First Advent) of Jesus literally fulfilled ancient prophecies. One prophecy even named the city in which He would be born:

"But as for you, Bethlehem Ephrata, too little to be among the clans of Judah, from you One will go forth for Me to be ruler in Israel. His goings forth are from long ago, from the days of eternity." Micah 5:2

We point to a literal interpretation of that and other passages as evidence for the authority and authorship of the Bible.

What about His Second Coming? The Second Coming prophecies mention Israel as a nation and race. It is unreasonable to say that the prophecies about his Second Coming (Second Advent) cannot be taken as literally as the prophecies of His First Coming in Bethlehem. We take them literally.

Israel's Future

Dispensationalists teach that Israel will be important in future events. There are numerous passages that talk about a future time when Jesus will reign in what appears to be a Theocracy. The capital city of that worldwide reign will be Jerusalem. Revelation chapter 21 gives us a time frame. The text repeatedly says that the reign will last for one thousand years. Dispensationalism interprets that literally. Dispensationalists say that in the future Jesus will reign on earth for 1,000 years and the Edenic Curse will be lifted from the earth. Dispensationalists call that time the Millennium or Millennial Kingdom. It is the time when we believe all the not-yet-fulfilled promises to Israel will finally be fulfilled.

But Israel becomes important before the 1,000 year Millennial Kingdom. Dispensational Theology teaches that in the future, Israel will be God's focus after Christ removes the Church to Heaven (1 Thessalonians 4:13-17) in what is called the Rapture. After the Rapture, God will restore Israel as the primary object of His work on earth. Revelation chapters 6-19 describe this time and speak of Israel often. It is a seven year period of death and destruction called The Tribulation. During this time, Israel will not reject Him as they did at His first coming. They will "look upon Me (Jesus) who they pierced" as prophesied in Zechariah 12:10-14. They will turn to Jesus as their Messiah! Those Jews and Gentiles that survive the Tribulation will inhabit the Millennial Kingdom. Jerusalem will be the capital city. Israel will be the leading nation, and representatives from all nations will come to Jerusalem to honor and worship the King, Jesus Christ. (Revelation 20:1-5)

What I have described is a Dispensational and Pre-millennial understanding of God's plan for Israel. The strongest support for this view is found in the clear teaching of Revelation 20:1-7, where Scripture says six times that Christ's kingdom will last 1,000 years.

Christ's rule involves Israel, not the Church. ***The church has not replaced Israel in God's plan.*** While God may be focusing His attention primarily on the church in this dispensation of grace, God has not forgotten Israel, and will one day restore her for the role He intended (Romans 11).

Israel, The Church, and the New Testament

The view that Israel and the Church are different is clearly taught in the New Testament. The Church is completely distinct from Israel, and the two terms are never to be confused or used interchangeably. We are taught from Scripture that the Church is an entirely new creation.

The Church has no relationship to the curses and blessings for national Israel. Those covenants, promises, and warnings are valid only for Israel. Israel has been preserved as a people in spite of severe persecution, but she has been temporarily set aside in God's program during the 2,000 years of this present dispensation. The Church is God's focus in this age.

In the New Testament, the Church is NOT Israel. There are 77 references to Israel in the NT and none of them refer to the Church. A good example is Rom. 10:1, "Brethren, my heart's desire and prayer to God for Israel is that they might be saved." It is ridiculous to replace Israel with "the Church." The Church is the body of saved believers, so how could Paul's prayer be for the Church to be saved?

Salvation Through the Ages

Though sometimes misunderstood, Dispensationalists believe that there has ALWAYS been only one plan of salvation for man. Salvation for Adam happened the same way that it happens today. God's gift of salvation in every age has always had three components:

- **By Grace**—God extending His grace toward man because sinful man is helpless to earn merit or favor in His sight.
- **Through Faith**—faith in the revealed Word of God.

- **Based on Blood**—the blood of animals was merely a "layaway payment" until the precious blood of Jesus Christ, the Lamb of God, paid the full debt sinful man owes. Hallelujah!

Want to Know More?

An excellent book for a comprehensive study of Dispensationalism is *There Really Is a Difference* by Renald E. Showers. In easy-to-understand language, Dr. Showers explores the differences between the Dispensational theology and other points of view.

Summary of Dispensational Theology

Dispensational Theology:

- Sees God's different way of ruling over men in the OT and NT.
- Interprets Scripture literally.
- Teaches that Israel will be important in future events.
- Says that Israel and the Church are distinctly different peoples.
- Believes that there has always been only one plan of salvation.
- Is not Replacement Theology.

What is Christian Replacement Theology?

Let's get acquainted with Replacement Theology. Simply stated, Replacement Theology is the belief that another people replace Israel in God's plan. It is the belief that the Jewish people are no longer God's chosen people. It says that God does not have any future plans for Israel as a race or political nation.

Replacement Theology teaches that the many biblical promises made to Israel have been transferred to the Christian Church. The prophecies of blessing and restoration of Israel to the Promised Land are "spiritualized" or "allegorized" into promises of God's blessing for the Church. Down through the centuries this view has sparked and fueled various misguided efforts including the Crusades. The

Crusades were terribly imprudent attempts to reclaim land that was supposedly given to the Church. If only they could have seen that God's promise of land for Israel was NOT transferred to any Christian Church, then much suffering and heartache could have been prevented!

A major problem with Replacement Theology is the continuing existence of the Jewish people throughout the centuries, and the re-birth of the political nation of Israel. If Israel has been condemned by God, and there is no future for the Jewish nation, how do we explain the supernatural survival of the Jewish people over the past 2000 years despite the many attempts to destroy them? How do we explain why and how Israel reappeared as a nation in the 20th century after not existing for 1900 years? God has a future plan for Israel.

Summary of Christian Replacement Theology

Replacement Theology teaches:

- Israel, the Jewish people and the land, has been replaced by the Christian Church in the purposes of God.
- The Jewish people are now no longer a "chosen people." They are no different from any other ethnic group.
- Apart from repentance, the new birth, and incorporation into the Church, the Jewish people have no future, no hope, and no calling in the plan of God.
- Since the Day of Pentecost in Acts 2, the term "Israel," as found in the Bible, now refers to the Church.
- The promises, covenants and blessings ascribed to Israel in the Bible have been taken away from the Jews and given to the Church, which has superseded them. However, the Jews are subject to the curses found in the Bible, as a result of their rejection of Christ.

Christian Replacement Theology teaches that the New Testament Church is "God's chosen people."

Mormons Tinker with Israel's Future

Early in Mormon history, while their theology was evolving, two differing lines of Mormon thought about the Jews developed. One sees Israel as a future political nation that will exist alongside a triumphant Mormon Church with capital cities in both Jerusalem and "Zion" (in America). This thinking seems to have come from men who converted to Mormonism from traditional Christian backgrounds. They brought a respect for Israel with them when they became Mormon.

The second line of thought is that there will be NO political nation of Israel. These Mormons see Israel as submitting to Joseph Smith's revelations and theology. Jews have to become Mormons.

There is a defining statement about this in their official theology. The basic Mormon beliefs are expressed by Joseph Smith in the "Thirteen Articles of Faith." Their 10th Article addresses their view regarding the Jews:

> "We believe in the literal gathering of Israel and in the restoration of the Ten Tribes; that Zion (the New Jerusalem) will be built upon the American continent; that Christ will reign personally upon the earth; and, that the earth will be renewed and receive its paradisiacal glory." (*Pearl of Great Price,* Articles of Faith)

On the surface, this looks almost acceptable to mainstream evangelical Christianity. But it is NOT! Mormons believe that they replace Israel. We see it in the teachings of their prophets. Remember, they believe that each President of their church is a 'living prophet' who speaks from God.

Let's look closely at the key word of their 10th Article of Faith.

Gathering

"Gathering" is the important word that we need to understand. What does "gathering" mean? Is this a gathering of Jews to be a political nation called Israel?

Mormons believe that Israel was "scattered forth upon the face of the earth because of their unbelief, their wickedness." (*Book of Mormon:* 3 Nephi 16:4) *The Book of Mormon* refers to these people as "members of the house of Israel", or "the covenant people of the Lord", or "the children of the covenant." (*Book of Mormon*: 1 Nephi 15:14, 3 Nephi 20:25-26)

Mormons believe that the "gathering" is not just a gathering in the Middle East; it is a ***gathering around the testimony of the restored (Mormon) gospel of Jesus Christ***!! Mormons believe that they actually become Jews. They replace the Jews as God's chosen people. LDS President, Joseph Fielding Smith, says,

> "Every person who embraces the gospel (of Jesus Christ)_ *becomes of the house of Israel*...The great majority of those who become members of the Church are literal descendants of Abraham through Ephraim, son of Joseph. Those who are not literal descendants of Abraham and Israel *must become such, and when they are baptized and confirmed they are grafted into the tree and are entitled to all the rights and privileges as heirs."* (Doctrines of Salvation"; McConkie; 3:246)

Another Mormon Church President, Spencer W. Kimball, explained it this way,

> "The *gathering of Israel is effected when the people of the faraway countries accept the gospel* and remain in their native lands..." ("Ensign"; May 1975; p. 4)

Of course he uses "gospel" to refer to the Mormon "good news" that the truth has been restored through Joseph. It is NOT a reference to the death, burial, and resurrection of Jesus Christ.

Another observation about Mormon Replacement Theology can be drawn from noting how they copied Jewish ideas. They have temples, rites, ceremonies, dietary laws, and even a priesthood. All of these ideas are easily found in the Old Testament. This is another indication that Mormons view themselves as replacements for Israel.

Joseph Smith claimed that Moses, the greatest Jewish leader apart from Jesus, appeared to him and gave him 'keys' to use in the re-gathering of Israel. (*Doctrine & Covenants* 110:11) It seems that Joseph wanted to be perceived as a modern Moses as well as a living prophet.

Christians strongly disagree with the LDS tenth article.

Mormon Summary

Mormons believe that they ARE Israel when they gather around their "restored Gospel" of Joseph Smith. They REPLACE Israel!

Muslims Tamper with Israel's Past

Simply stated, Muslims attempt to rewrite the history of the Jewish people. They claim that Abraham's son Ishmael, not Isaac, is the son of promise. This revision is really another form of Replacement Theology discussed above. Again, Replacement Theology is the fingerprint that matches with the Mormons.

We must understand what Muslims believe about Israel and God's promises to Israel. The story goes back to Abraham.

> ***The Bible says,*** "And Abraham said unto God, O that Ishmael might live before thee! And God said, Sarah thy wife shall bear thee a son indeed; and thou shall call his name Isaac: and I will establish my covenant with him for an everlasting covenant, and with his seed after him." Genesis 17:18-19
>
> ***The Qur'an says,*** "Also mention in the Book [the story of] Ishmael: He was [strictly] true to what he promised, and he was a messenger [and] a prophet." S 19:54

Abraham's wife, Sarah, was frustrated with her inability to have a child. She had God's promise that she would become pregnant but she was impatient with God's timing. She asked Abraham to give her a child through Hagar, their Egyptian maidservant. Genesis 16:1-2

Hagar submitted to this culturally acceptable practice. She was "married" to Abraham and became pregnant. Her pregnancy made her feel superior to Sarah. Friction between these women developed. Polygamy always leads to heartache and trouble. When it was too much for Hagar, she ran into the desert. In the dire circumstances of the desert, God instructed her to return to Sarah. God promised,

"I will multiply thy seed exceedingly, that it shall not be numbered for multitude." Genesis 16:10

Thirteen years later, when Abraham was 99 years of age, God appeared to him and announced that his wife Sarah would bear him a son and that they would call him Isaac. It would be through Isaac that God would establish His covenant. Abraham struggled with this because he loved Ishmael dearly and desired that Ishmael be his heir to the birthright blessings.

God's plan was that the blessings would be given to Isaac, the child of promise. God denied Ishmael the birthright. However, God reassured Abraham that Ishmael would father a large nation of people.

Jews, Christians, and Muslims all attempt to follow the steps of Abraham as a father of the faith. God made an everlasting covenant with him:

"I will establish my covenant between me and thee and thy seed after thee in their generations for an everlasting covenant, to be a God unto thee." Genesis 17:7

This covenant between God and Abraham included blessings, a homeland, and "seed." The seed represents a vast multitude of blessed descendents that have an impact on the entire world. The issue is that both Jews and Muslims claim to be the chosen descendents of Abraham. Each is claiming that the blessings, homeland, and seed belong to them. Each side says, "We are the true descendents of Father Abraham!" In one sense, this is true. Both Jews and

Muslims descend from the bloodline of Abraham. The real issue is which line of descendents can claim the special and unique blessings God promised to Abraham's seed. Muslims say that the blessings were passed through Ishmael. Jews say the blessings were passed through Isaac.

Muslim Summary

Muslims rewrite the history of the Jewish people and claim that Ishmael, not Isaac, is the son of promise. Muslims say that they, not Israel, are the rightful heirs to all the wealth and blessing bestowed upon Abraham's promised descendents.

Chapter Conclusion

The Bible recognizes Israel in the past, present and future.
Muslims replace Israel in the past.
Mormons replace Israel in the future.
Replacement is their matching fingerprint!

Chapter 8

Questions for Discussion

1. How could you start a conversation about Jesus with a Jewish person?
2. If a Jewish person converts, is he or she a Christian Jew or a Jewish Christian?
3. How important is a government official's stance on Israel?
4. Does a literal interpretation include figurative language?
5. How were OT saints saved By Grace? Through Faith? Based on Blood?

Chapter 9

Calling Witnesses to Mormons and Muslims

Sharing the Gospel with a Mormon or a Muslim can be a fearful experience. I hope this short chapter will help believers say, "I CAN DO THIS!"

God is looking for men and women who are willing to serve as witnesses to both Mormons and Muslims. A witness should tell the truth, the whole truth and nothing but the truth. Mormons and Muslims need to hear the truth about who God is. They need to hear the whole truth about God's love for them that caused Him to send Jesus to die in their place. They also need to hear the nothing-but-the-truth part – that salvation is found in nothing but Jesus Christ.

The Bible calls us to be witnesses to all men. We are commanded to go and "make disciples of all the nations." (Matthew 28:19-20) That command includes Mormons and Muslims. How can we be a witness to them? First, let's build a strong foundation for witnessing. Then we will look at ten "golden rules" for witnessing.

The Foundation for Taking the Witness Stand

The foundation includes understanding the Gospel, understanding the enemy, and gaining the confidence we can have when sharing our faith.

The Gospel is Good News!

The Gospel is **good news**. It is the good news that God offers salvation from sin. God extends this offer to all men–Mormons and Muslims. In a narrow sense, the Gospel is the good news about what Jesus did for mankind. In a broad sense, it encompasses the total plan of God to redeem people from sin, death, Satan, and the curse that now covers the earth.

In 1 Corinthians 15:1-7, the apostle Paul summarizes the most basic ingredients of the gospel message. The heart of the gospel is the death, burial, resurrection, and appearances of the resurrected Christ. You can see these four ingredients in the verses below.

> "Now I make known to you, brethren, the gospel...that Christ died for our sins according to the Scriptures, and that He was buried, and that He was raised on the third day according to the Scriptures, and that He appeared...to all the apostles." 1 Corinthians 15:1-7

An even closer look shows that the purest essence of the Gospel is a two-fold message: (1) Christ died for our sins and (2) He was raised on the third day. The other two elements are important verifications. The fact that He was buried *verified His death*, and the fact that He appeared to others *verified His resurrection*.

The term *gospel* is found ninety-nine times in the New American Standard Bible. In the Greek New Testament, *gospel* is the translation of the Greek noun *euangelion* and means "good news." It is also a verb, *euangelizo,* and means "to bring or announce good news." Both the noun and verb forms show us that we have good news to share with Mormons and Muslims!

Satan opposes the Gospel

The second feature of the foundation is knowing that we have an enemy. The enemy is Satan and he does not want the good news to get out. We need to remember that the world, not just our Mormon and Muslim friends, is blinded to the Gospel. Satan wants to keep people from understanding the Gospel of Christ.

"And even if our gospel is veiled, it is veiled to those who are perishing, in whose case the god of this world has blinded the minds of the unbelieving so that they might not see the light of the gospel of the glory of Christ, who is the image of God." 2 Corinthians 4:3-4

Do Not Be Ashamed of the Gospel

The third trait is that we should be eager, not ashamed, to share the gospel. Never hesitate to share it. Why? The gospel is the power of God unto salvation. Communicating the gospel is unleashing power. God sets to work in the hearer when he hears the message.

"For I am not ashamed of the gospel, for *it is the power of God* for salvation to everyone who believes…For in it the righteousness of God is revealed from faith to faith; as it is written, 'BUT THE RIGHTEOUS man SHALL LIVE BY FAITH.'" Romans 1:16-17

Even extremist religious terrorists can be changed by the Gospel power of God! *True Story*: A religious terrorist from the Middle East was literally on his way to Syria to murder Christians. He was a veteran at killing and had personally witnessed a Christian being murdered by a mob. He hated the infidels who dared say his religion was not the truest on earth. He longed to shed their blood. But, when he came face to face with the truth of Christ, he became a Christian! He was changed from a terrorist to a missionary. The story did not make any cable news channels, but it is readily accessible. You will be encouraged if you read it for yourself. [1]

Trust the God of the Gospel as You Witness

The fourth plank in the foundation is to trust God, not your method. Paul is our example. He and the others who spread the good news did not depend on their looks, their learning, their magnetic personalities, nor their speaking skills. They prayed for the hearers and then proclaimed the message. They preached the gospel with conviction, resting in the fact they were preaching the powerful life-giving truth of God. They were fortified by the fact that the supernatural ministry of the Spirit of God would work His will in the hearers.

We need to do our best in the delivery while we trust God to work in the life of the hearer. We deliver the news. God works with it. We use our lips to say the words while we trust the Holy Spirit to do a work in the heart of the hearer. The internal work is done by the Spirit of God changing the heart to respond inwardly to the Gospel message. The Spirit of God woos. The Father draws men to Christ. The Spirit of God causes the heart of the sinner to be willing to repent of his sins and believe on the Lord Jesus. One passage that should give us comfort and confidence is John 6:44. Jesus said,

"No one can come to Me unless the Father who sent Me draws him."

It may be helpful to think of the Gospel as a good radiation. Our job is to expose people to it. It will have its effect according to the will of God. The Bible teaches that the Spirit, not the witness, graciously causes a sinner to cooperate, to believe, to repent, to come freely and willingly to Christ. God's grace will be irresistible to the ones He is calling! We are just the messengers. Thus, salvation of a Mormon or Muslim (or anyone) is all of God and not of man in any way, shape, or form. He deserves all the credit, praise, and glory.

Ten Fingerprint Principles for Witnesses

The rules match the fingerprint analogy because they apply to both groups, and there are ten–as in one for each finger. There are Ten Golden Rules for witnessing encounters with Mormons or Muslims. These are the ten fingerprints that every witness should leave behind.

1. Do not insult.

- Mormons are taught to respond to attacks leveled by Christians. It can be disarming to them when you do not charge in and attack.

- When witnessing to a Muslim do not insult Mohammed or the Qur'an. This kind of talk will build barriers that are not easily overcome.

2. Avoid arguments.

- Mormons do not respond to arguments over inconsistencies in their doctrines and past practices, such as polygamy. There is plenty of ammunition for arguments but they should be avoided. Remember, the Mormon sees the freshest revelation from Salt Lake as the most authoritative. You may win the argument, but you won't win the Mormon.
- A Muslim might be prone to argue about things like the Crusades. Be prepared to give adequate but short answers and seek to get back to the subject. Don't start an argument. If an argument starts to flare up, smother it.

3. Avoid anger.

Don't fall into the whirlpool of an emotionally charged discussion. Remember, Proverbs 15:1 says, "A soft answer turns away wrath..." Give soft answers and keep the conversation going in the right direction.

4. Be respectful of God as you talk about Him.

A Muslim expects you to act respectfully when you talk of God. Do not lounge back and prop your feet up. Do not be flippant or too casual. A Muslim will be more apt to listen carefully if you convey that your relationship to God is sacred. Show by your behavior that you are in awe of your God. Do not put your Bible on the floor or put a cup of coffee on top of it. A Muslim will notice.

5. Speak to one person at a time if possible.

- Mormon missionaries usually go out two at a time. This is so that one can hold the other accountable. If possible, try to befriend them as individuals.
- For Muslims, their family, friends, and relationships are very important. They are likely to "toe the line" of their faith when in a group. Again, if possible, try to befriend them and speak to them as individuals. Invite them to your home. Feed them.

6. Be a friend first.

Don't give the impression that you care about the person only if they become a Christian. Seek to be real, and develop a real friendship. Muslim cultures put a high value on friendships and time spent together. You may be the first Christian they know. See them as people, not prospects. Ask about their homeland and their customs. Listen with the same openness you want from them.

7. Stay on the subject.

Stick to the subject: we are all sinners who need Jesus; we cannot save ourselves. Avoid comparisons and self-justifications. The person may bring up a hot topic to move away from a convicting point. Don't bite at the hot topic. Stick to the point of sharing the truth.

8. Avoid Politics.

Muslims will be offended if you focus on Israel, the Palestinians, or other political subjects. Say something like, "I am very sorry for the suffering of the Palestinians and the Israelis. The people responsible for that suffering will have to answer to God."

9. Quote and refer to the Bible freely.

- With Mormons, it might be better to use a King James Version of Scripture. Remember, they accept it and even include it in their Quad.
- Islamic culture responds to stories. Your witness will be helped if you are versed in the Bible narratives. Use them easily and freely as illustrations and conversing points. Show the person that you "know your stuff" about the Bible. Hiding God's Word in the heart is good for both the witness and the hearer.

10. Answer their objections.

Obviously, it is not good to act like a know-it-all. However, if possible, anticipate their objections and be prepared with an adequate answer. Remember that you do not want to fall into the trap of being sidetracked.

Read good books, like this one, that provide more information about what they believe.

Chapter Conclusion

Don't bash Mormons and Muslims. Speak the truth in love. Love them to Jesus!

Notes

Chapter 1

[1] Joseph Smith said this at the end a speech in the public square at Far West, Missouri on October 14, 1838. This quote is from Fawn M. Brodie's book, *No Man Knows My History*, second edition, (New York: Alfred A. Knopf, 1971), p. 230–231.

[2] "*A Message of Friendship,*" written for the Foundation for Apologetic Information and Research by David Stewart in 2003. It can be accessed at *www.fairlds.org*.

Chapter 2

[1] Mormons practice *predatory proselytizing* and seek to convert members of other denominations. They capitalize on those who are ungrounded in the truth. Mormon missionaries are glad to find recent converts to Christianity. To a newly converted Presbyterian they might say, "You have been told about the Old Testament and the New Testament. We have Another Testament of Jesus Christ."

Chapter 3

[1] World Religions by Warren Matthews

[2] Introduction to World Religions by Christopher Partridge

[3] We will refer to Joseph Smith Jr. simply as Joseph or Joseph Smith. Please do not confuse Joseph Smith Jr, the founder, with Joseph Fielding Smith, a later president of the LDS church.

Chapter 4

[1] *The Qur'an and Its Interpreters*, Vol. II *The House of Imran.* 1992 State University of New York Press, Albany, p. 165.

[2] John Elder, *Prophets, Idols and Diggers* [New York; Bobs Merrill, 1960], p. 16

[3] E. M. Blaiklock, editor's preface, *New International Dictionary of Biblical Archeology* Grand Rapids, MI; Regency Reference Library/ Zondervan, 1983, pp. vii-viii)

[4] Quoted by J. A. Thompson, *The Bible and Archeology* Grand Rapids, MI; Eerdmans, 1975, p. 5)

Chapter 9

[1] Acts chapters 9, 22, and 26. Compare these with I Timothy 1:15!

Printed in the United States
201514BV00005B/13-21/P